How to Draw Koi Fishes Step-by-Step Guide

Best Koi Fish Drawing Book for You and Your Kids

BY

ANDY HOPPER

Copyright Notes

Table of Contents

Introduction

Kids have this intense desire to express themselves the ways they know how to. During their formative years, drawing all sorts is on top of their favorite things to do. You ought to encourage as it boosts their creativity and generally advances their cognitive development.

This book is written to give you and your kids the smoothest drawing experience with the different guides and instructions on how to draw different kinds of objects and animals. However, you should note that drawing, like everything worthwhile, requires a great deal of patience and consistency. Be patient with your kids as they wade through the tips and techniques in this book and put them into practice. Now, they will not get everything on the first try, but do not let this deter them. Be by their side at every step of the way and gently encourage them. In no time, they will be perfect little creators, and you, their trainer.

Besides, this is a rewarding activity to do as it presents you the opportunity of hanging out with your kids and connecting with them in ways you never knew was possible. The book contains all the help you need, now sit down with them and help them do this.

That is pretty much all about it - we should start this exciting journey now, shouldn't we?

How to Draw A Koi 1

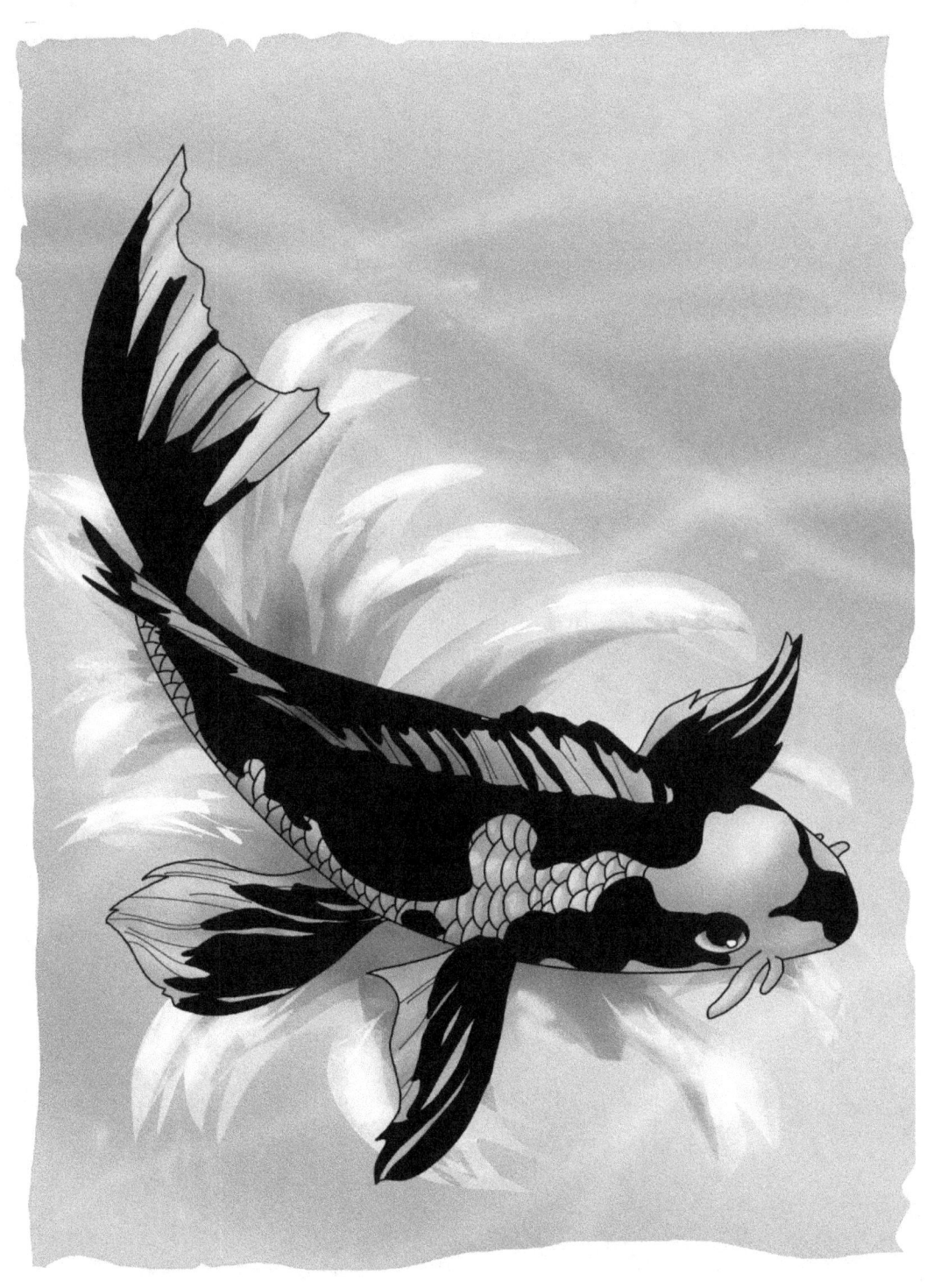

Step 1.

Make a stretched out peanut shape for the body.

Step 2.

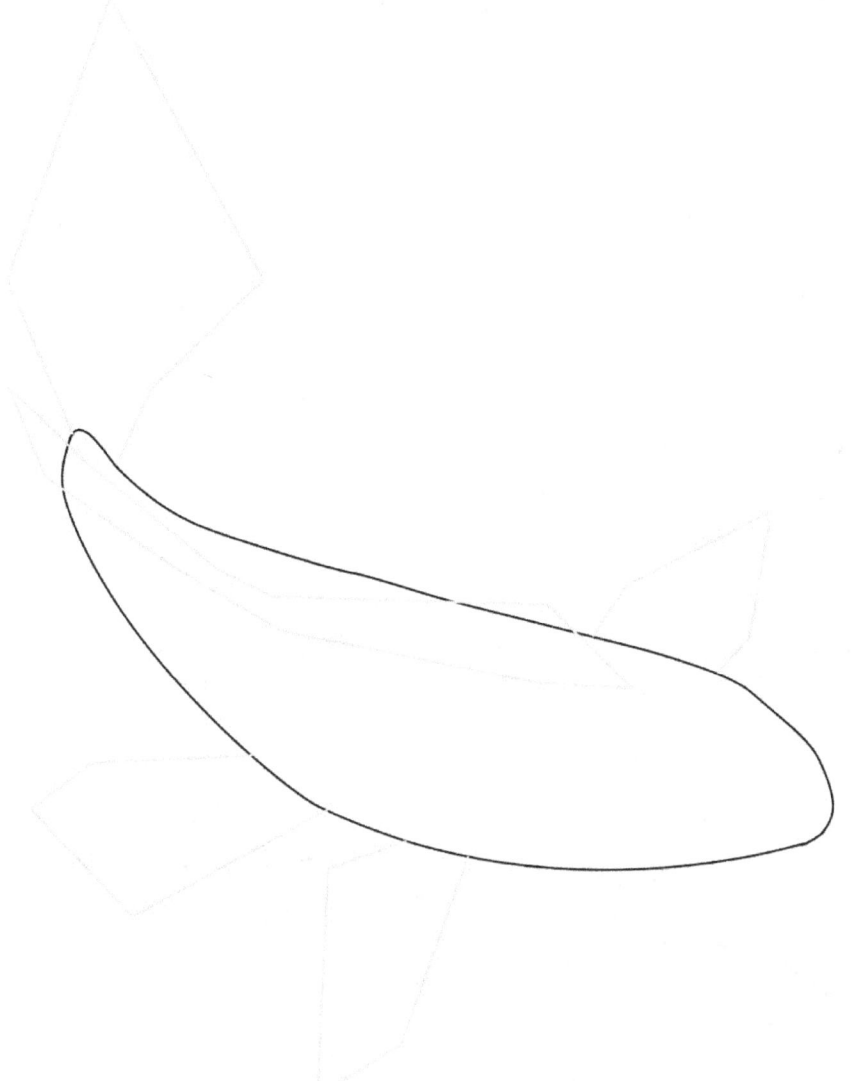

Add the outline of the dorsal fins, back fin and the tail fin as in the example.

Because of the perspective, we can only see 3 of the 4 dorsal fins.

[7]

Step 3.

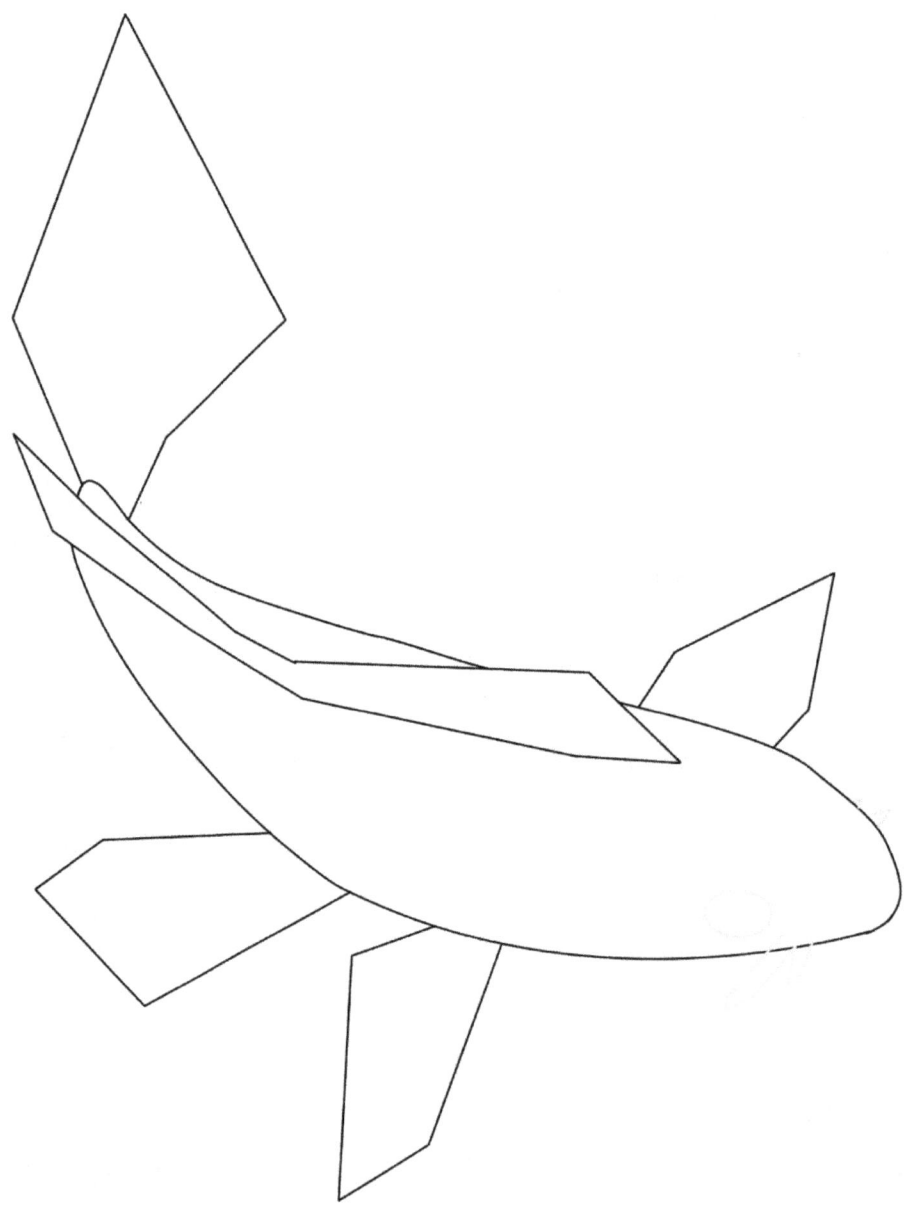

Add the appendixes to the snout and the eye to the head.

Step 4.

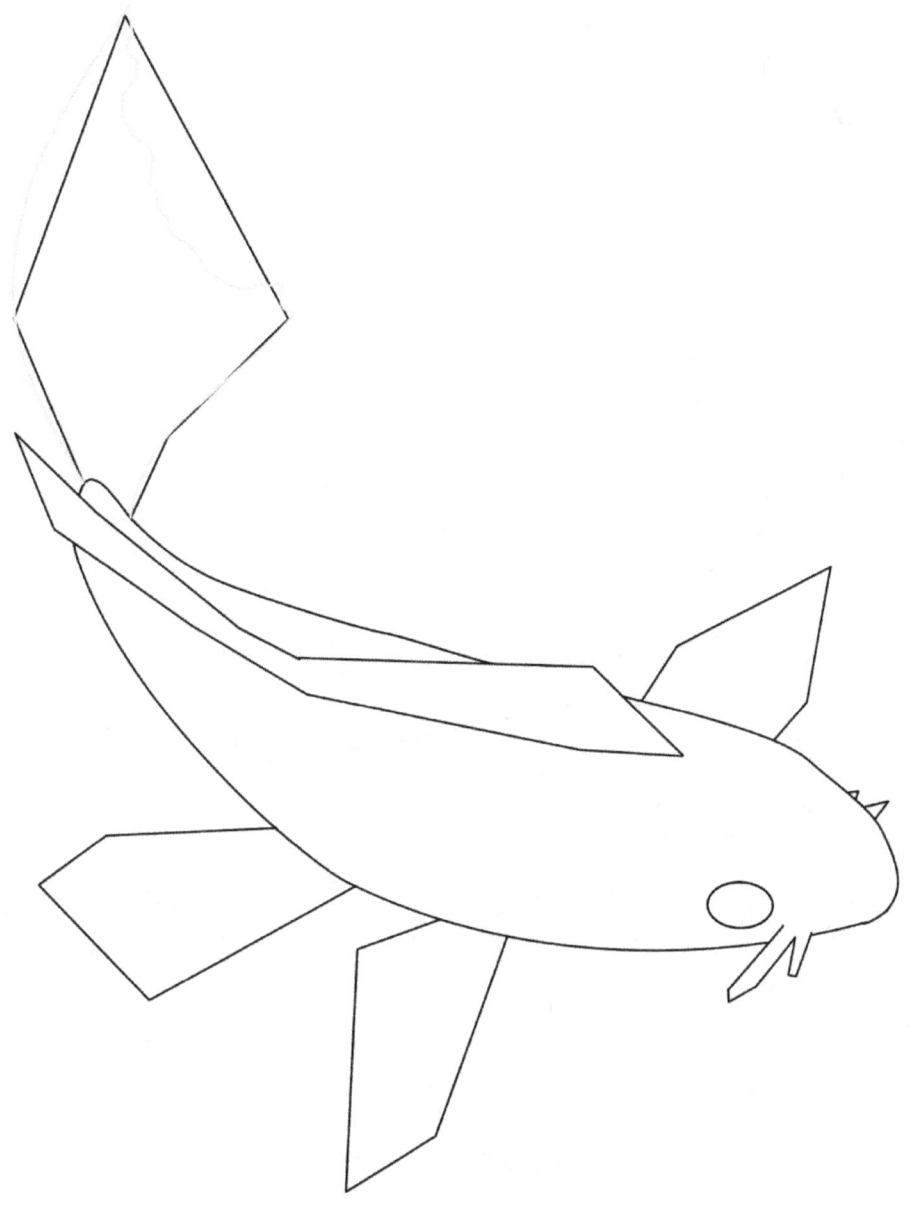

Start by redrawing the outline of the tailfin.

Step 5.

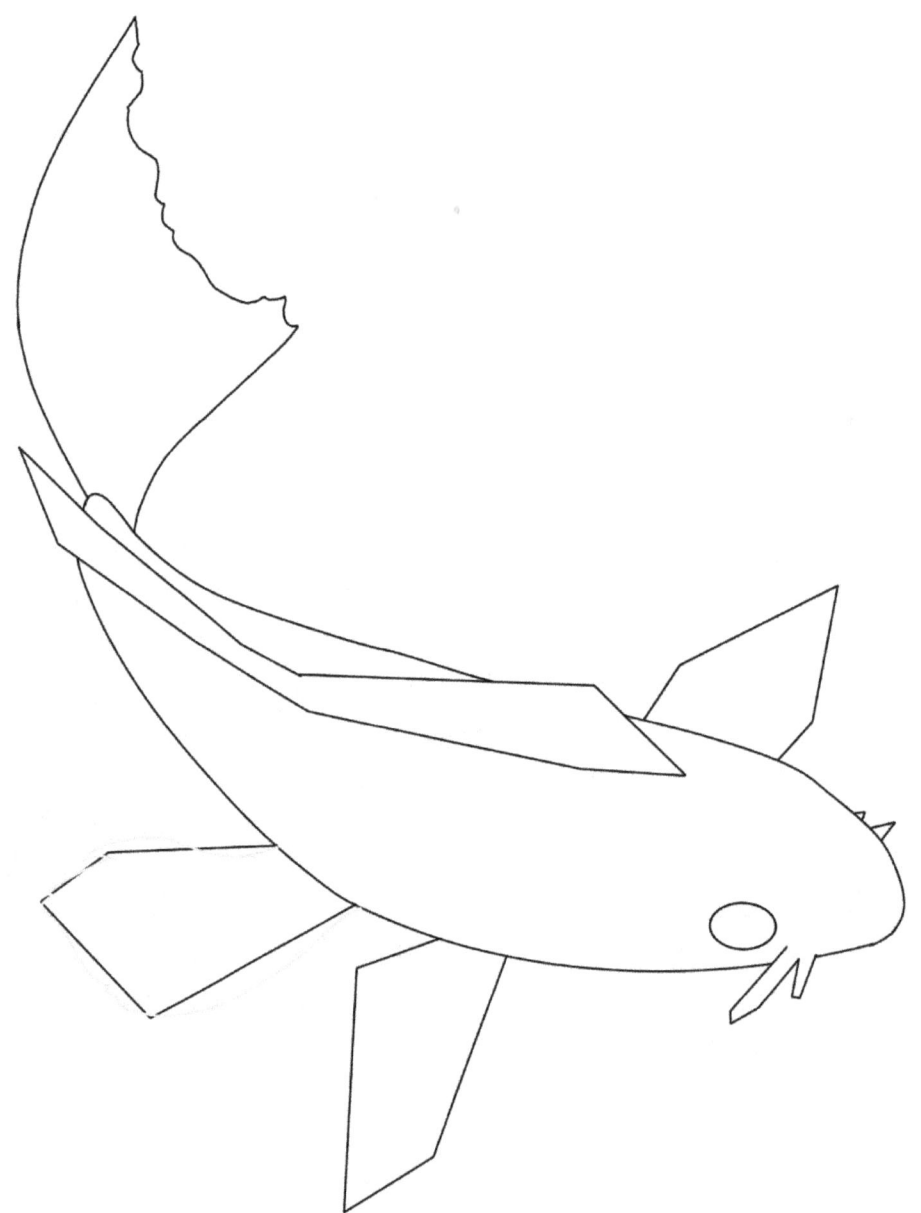

Then proceed with the lonely fin at the back of the body.

Step 6.

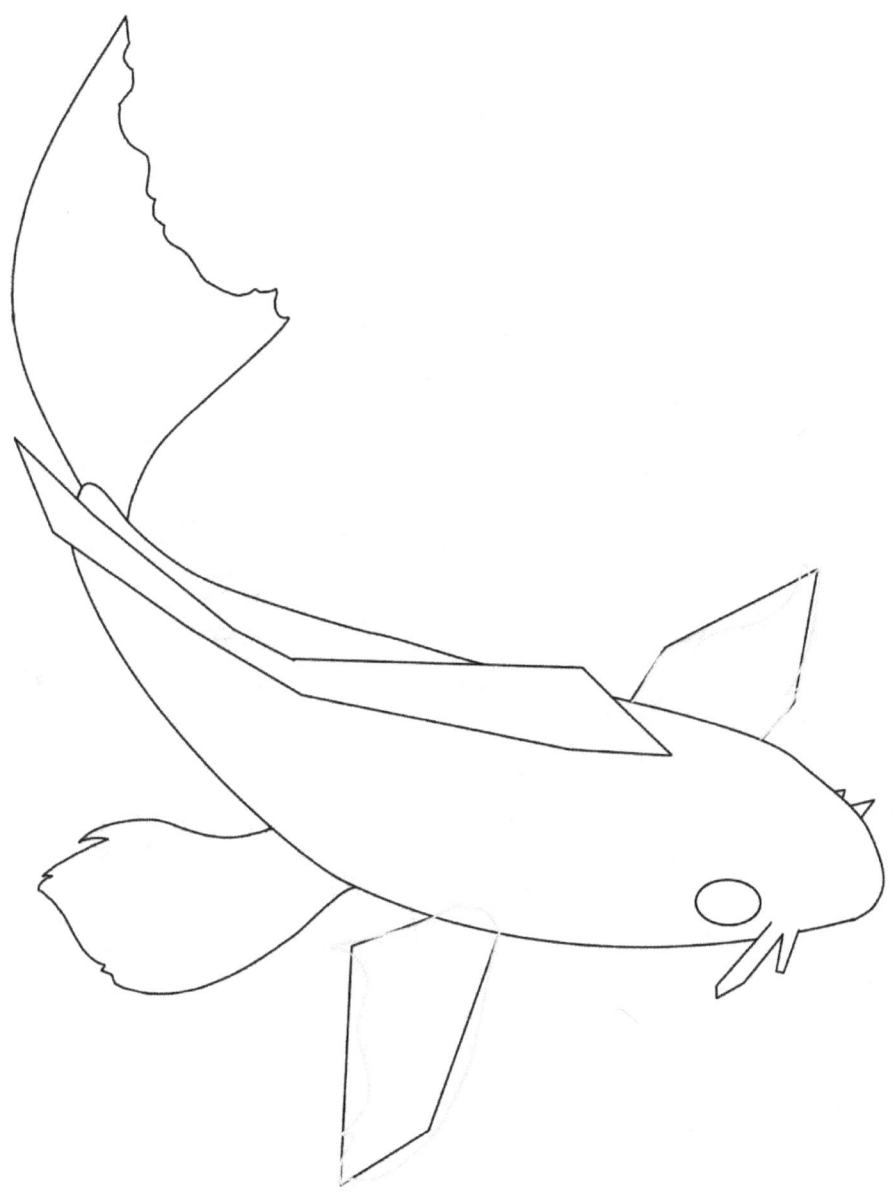

Lastly the fins on the front need to be redrawn as in the example.

Step 7.

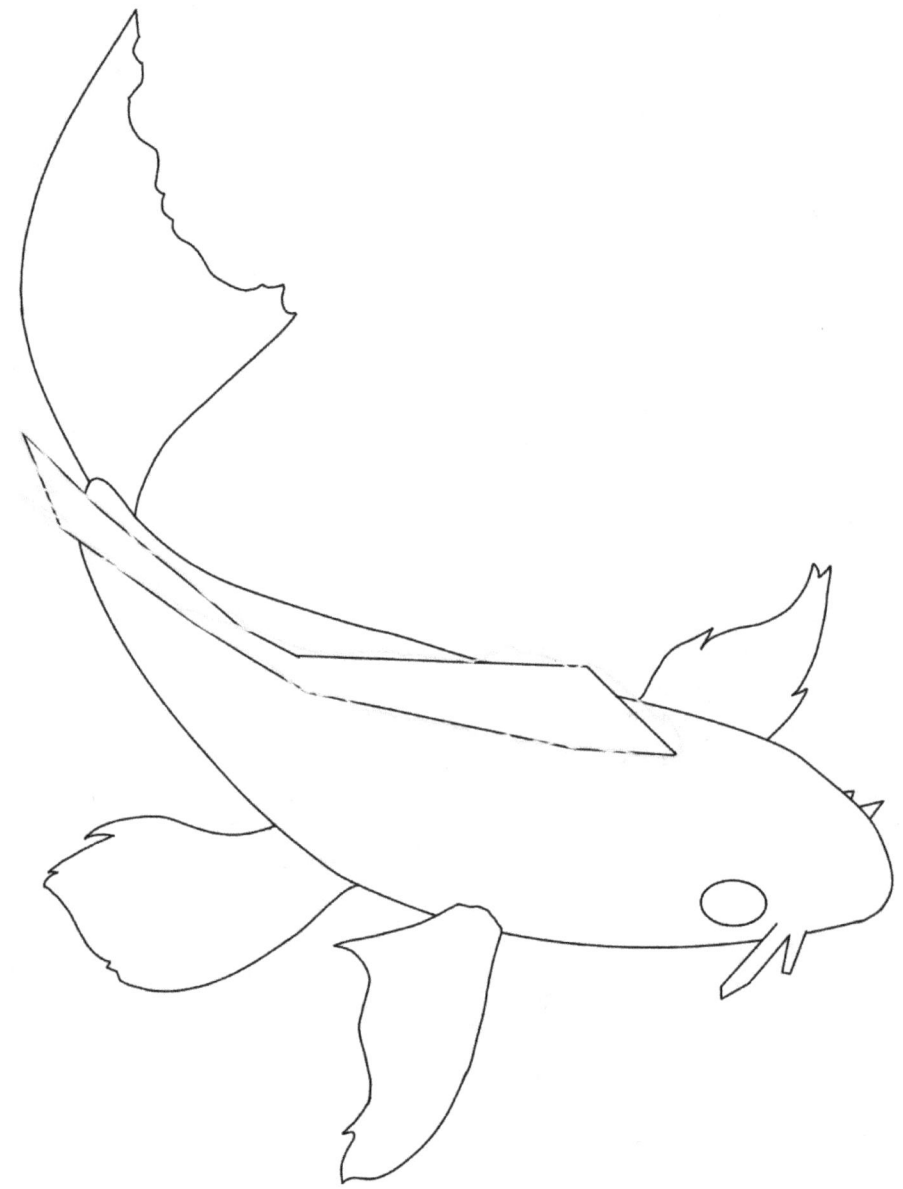

The back fin swirls in the water as it bends with the motion of the body.

Because of this, we see part of the right side in the front and that of the left side at the back.

Step 8.

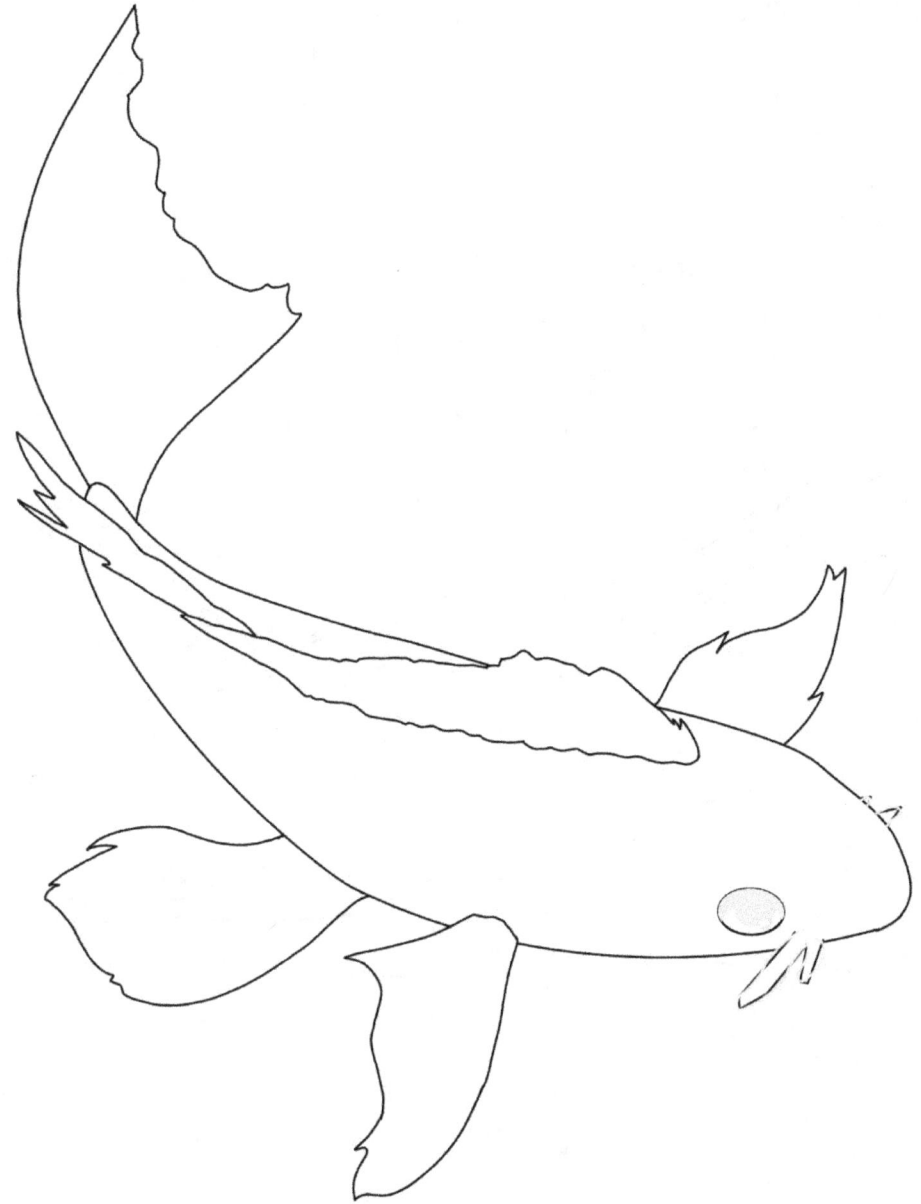

Redraw the appendixes to make the smoother and complete
the eye.

Step 9.

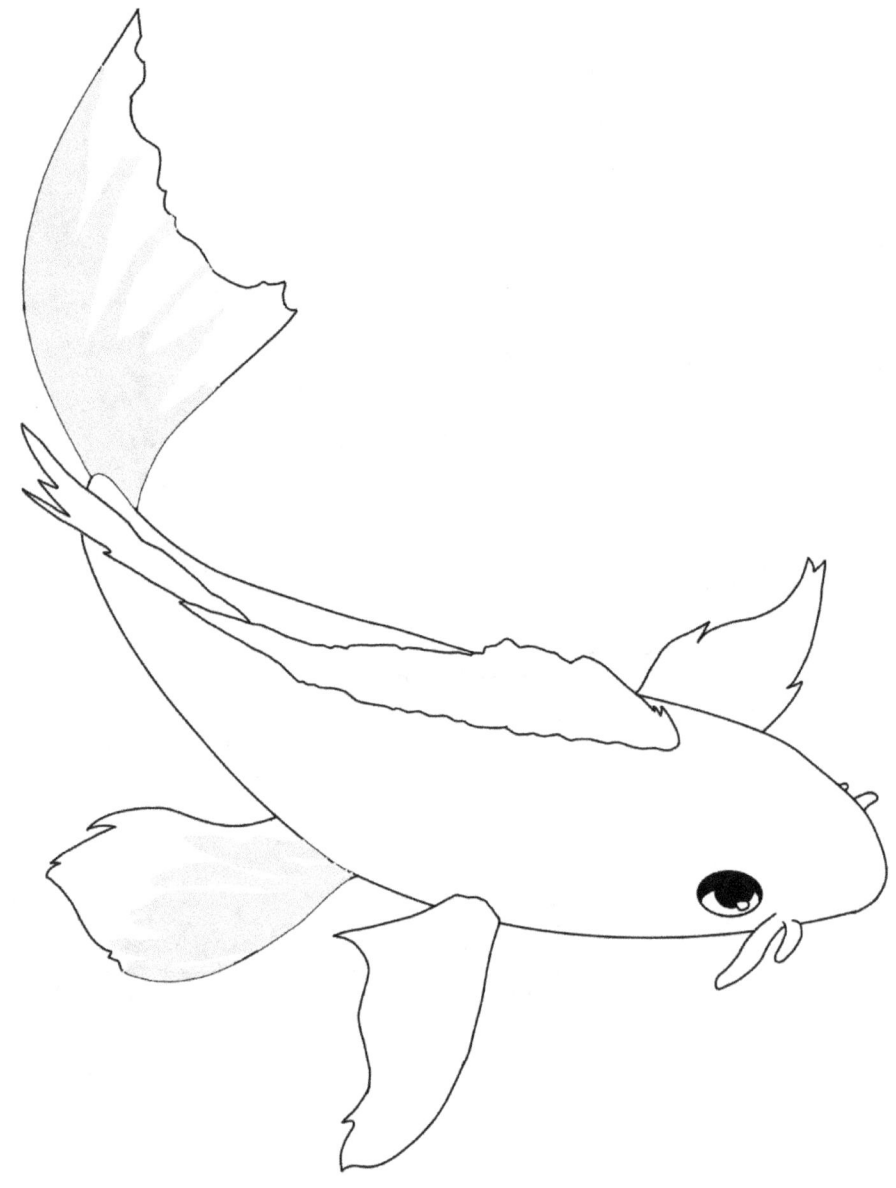

Our Koi has black spots on its fins. Similar in shape as the spots on a cow.

Follow the example to help you create the spot in motion with the fin.

Step 10.

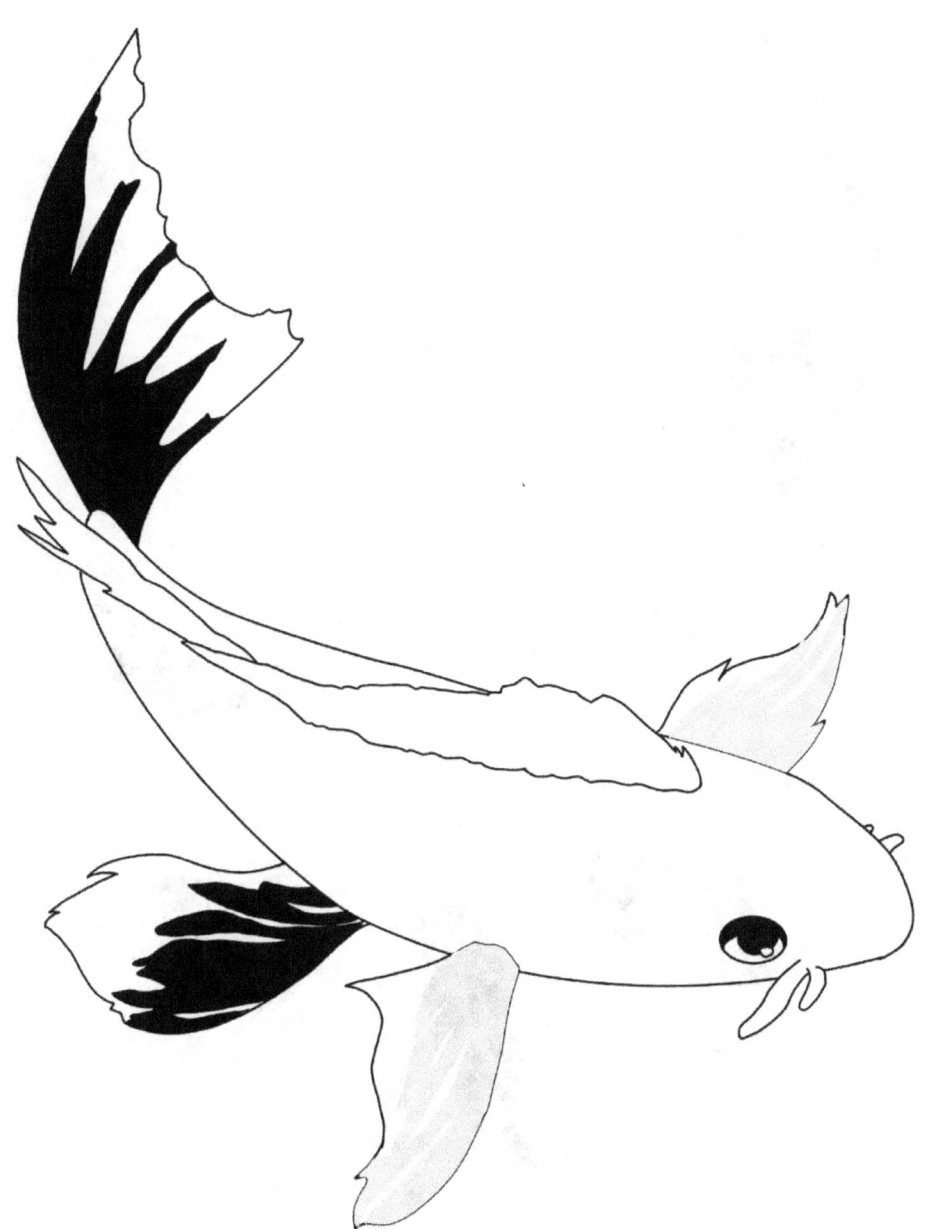

Do the same to the fins in the front of the body.

Step 11.

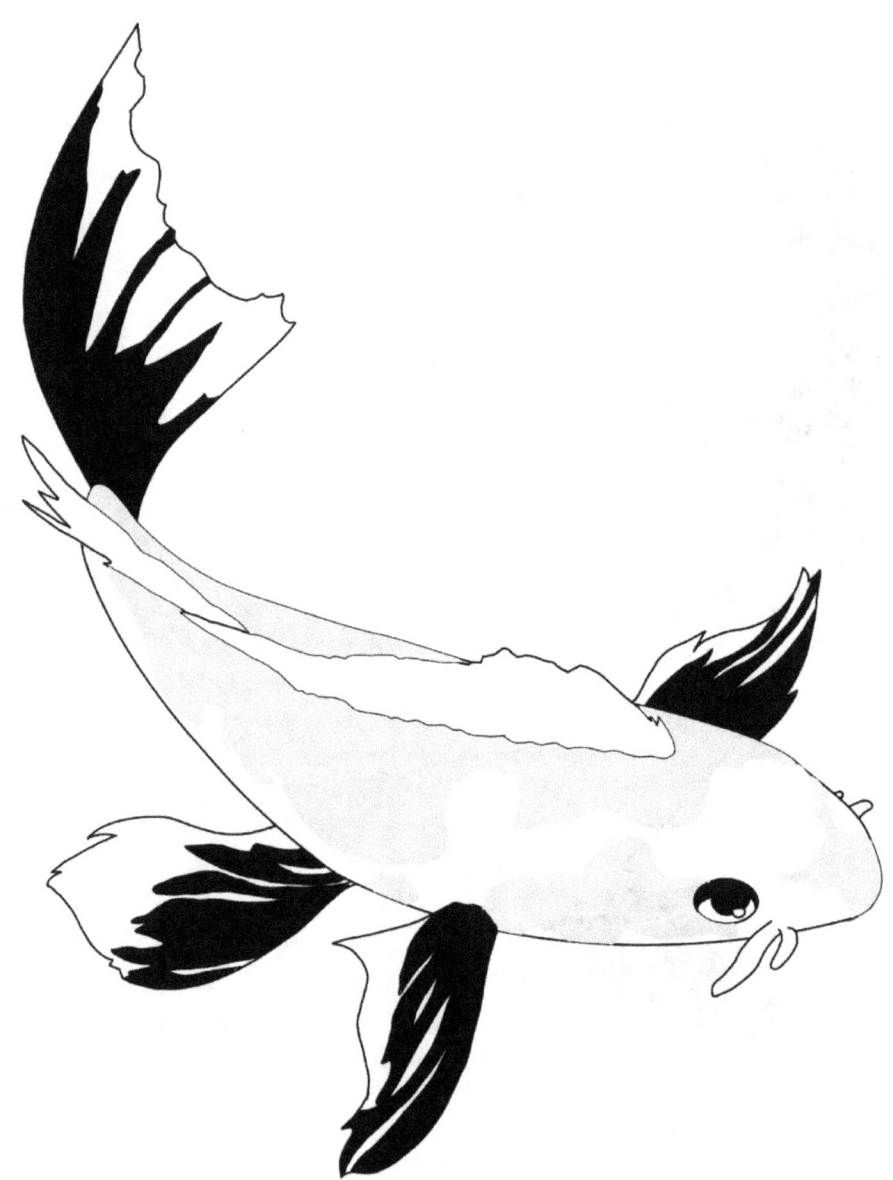

Now it's time to make some ink-like blobs on the body,
matching it with the spots on the fins.

Step 12.

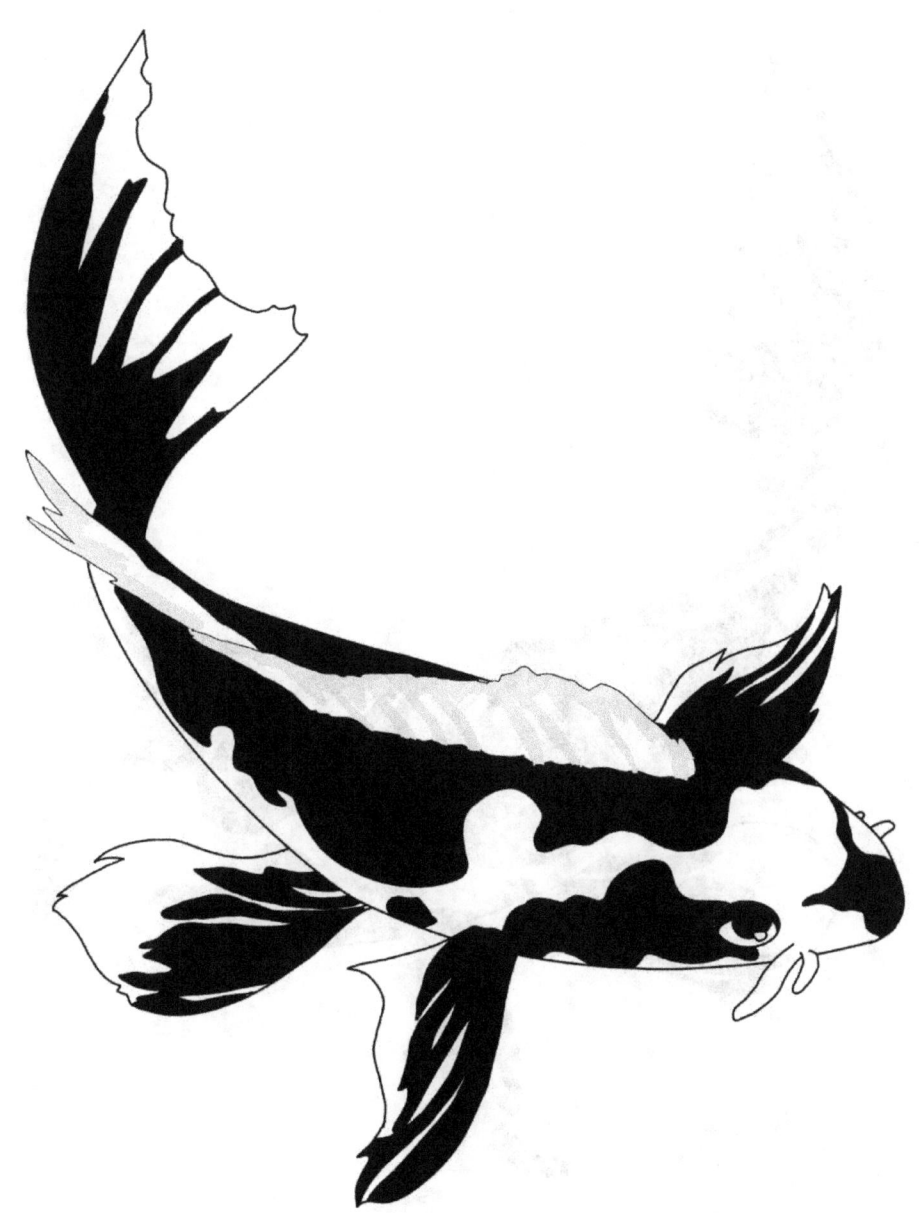

Lastly, at the spots on the fin on the back of the body.

Step 13.

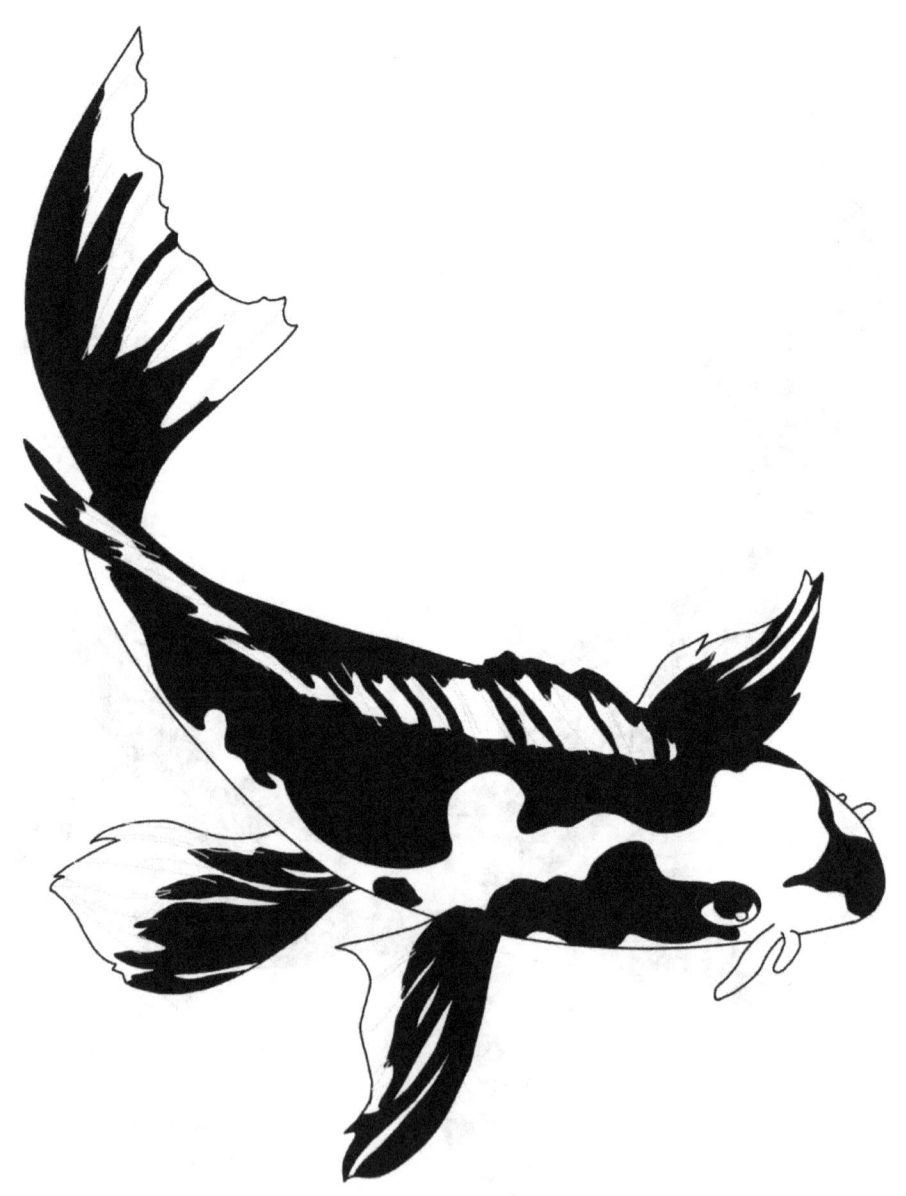

Add lines inside the fins to give them more detail. Add as many
as you please.

Step 14.

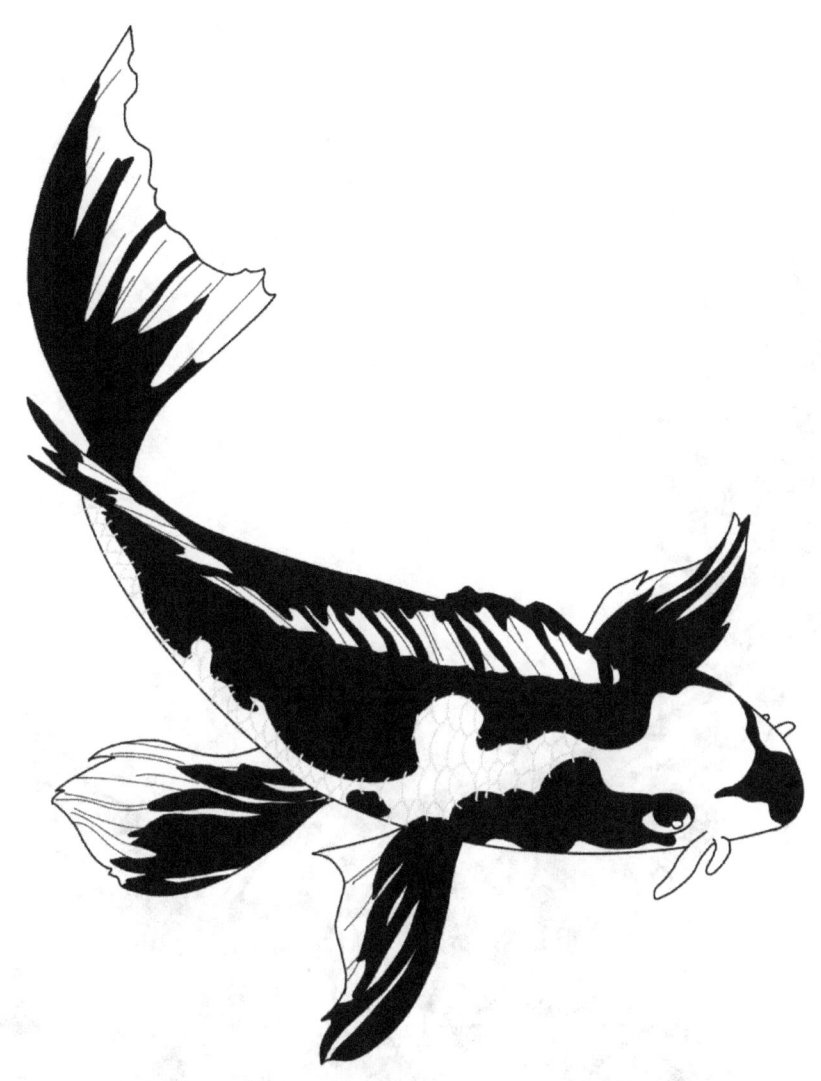

Now it's time for the scales.

Because of the anatomy of a Koi fish, the scales are almost completely on the body and not on the head.

Look at the example and start adding small C-shapes on top of each other. Make sure you follow the motion of the body.

Step 15.

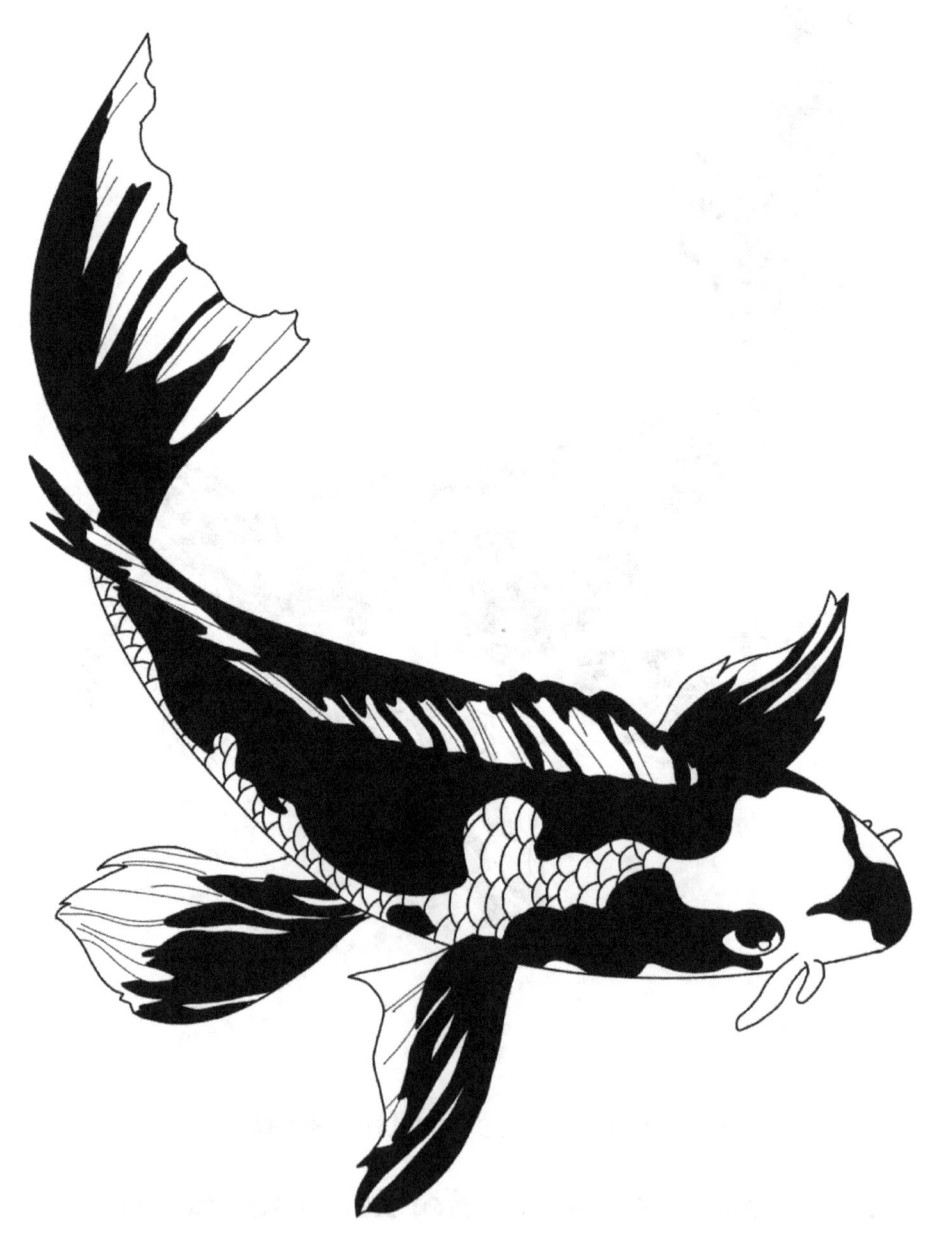

All done! It's time to color!

Step 16.

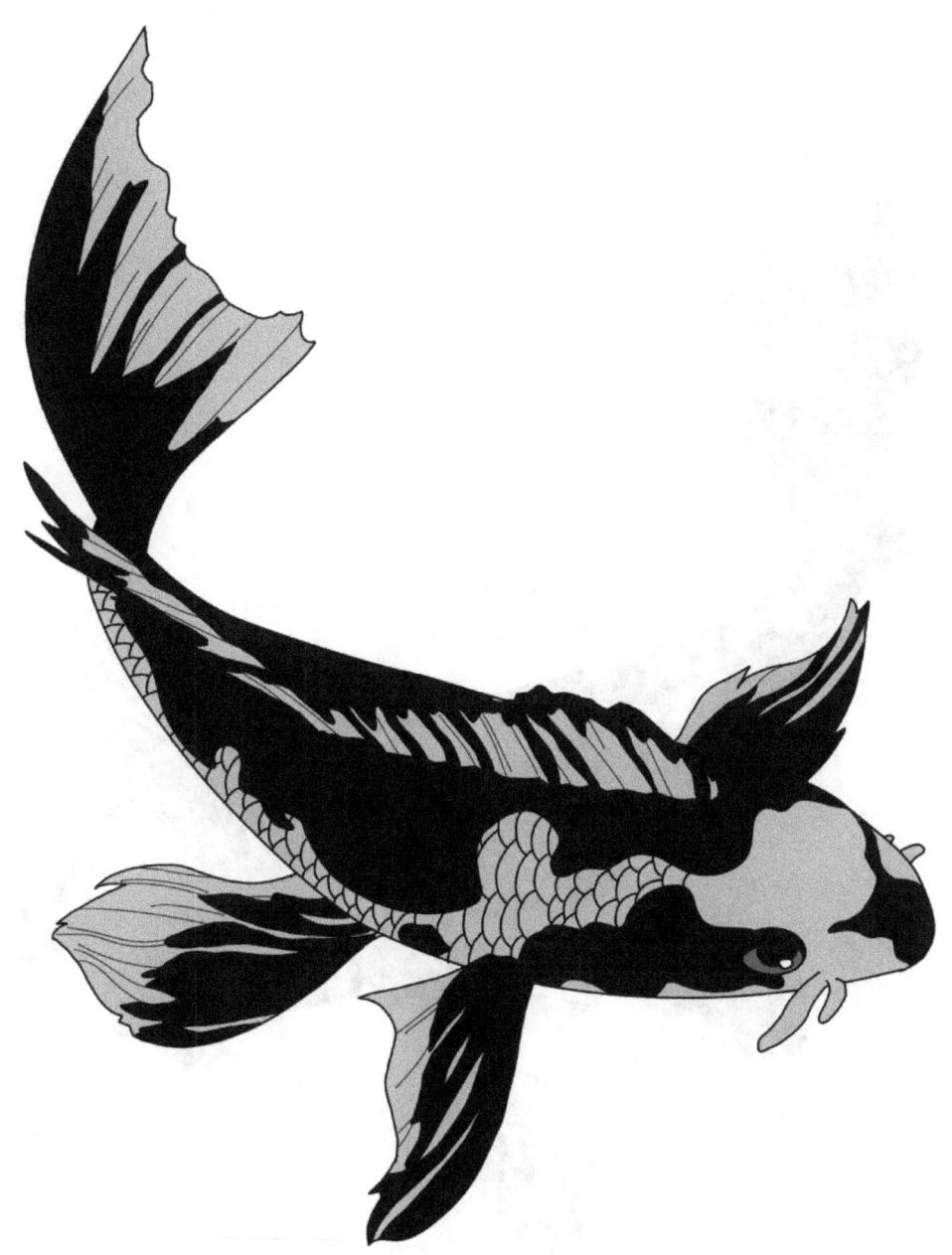

Our Koi is completely orange.

His eye is green.

Step 17.

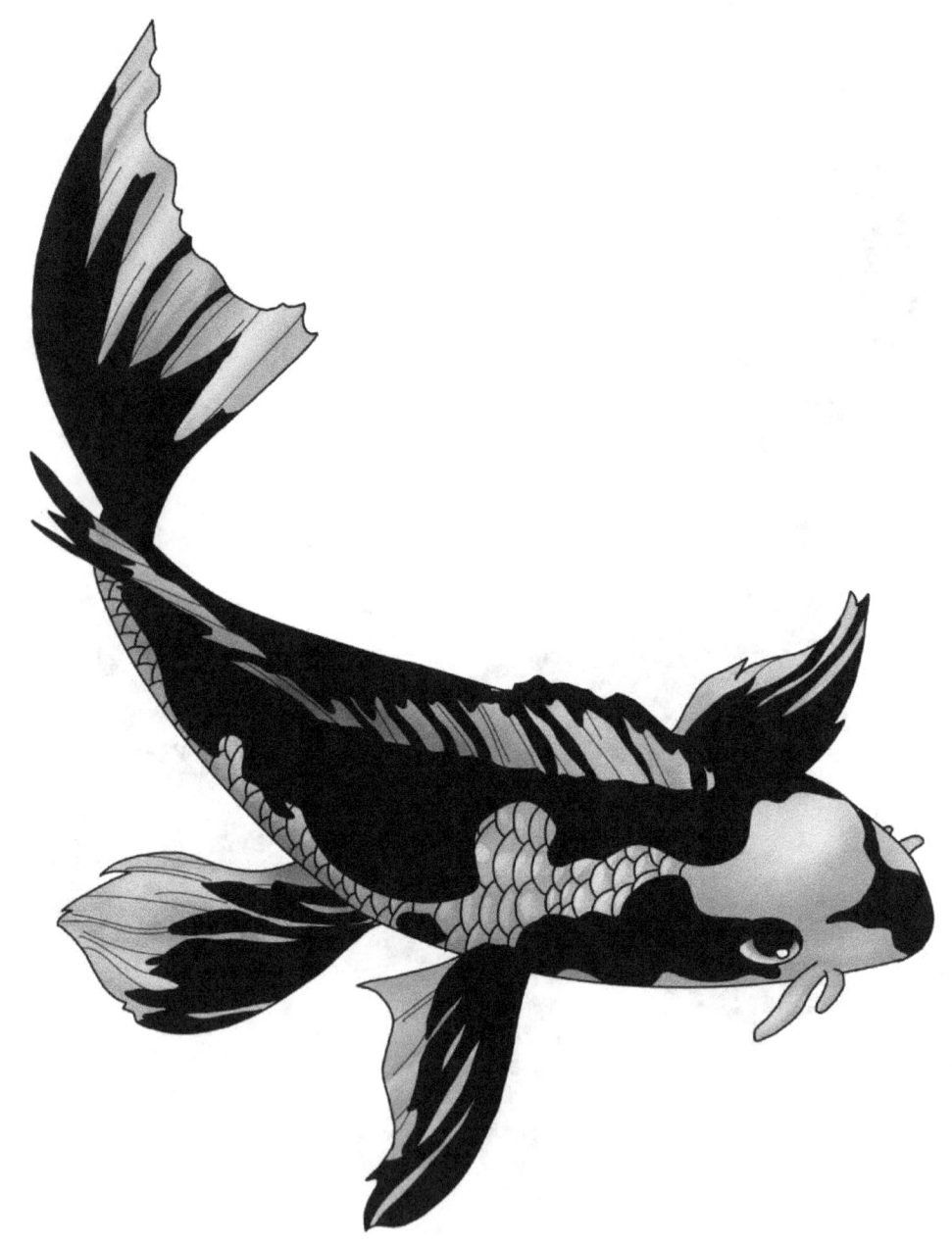

Add shadow and highlights to give our koi volume.

Step 18.

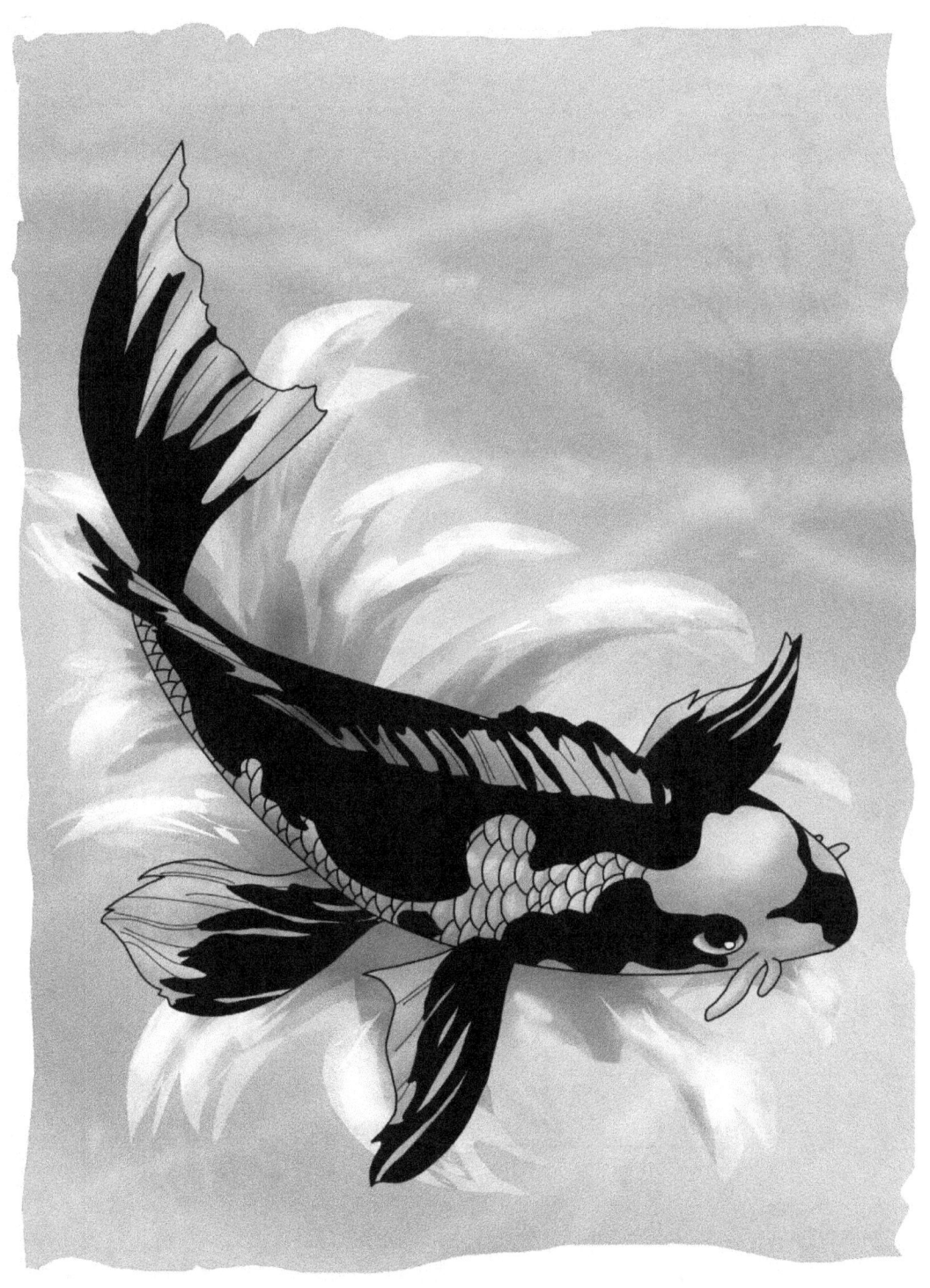

Colored version.

Step 19.

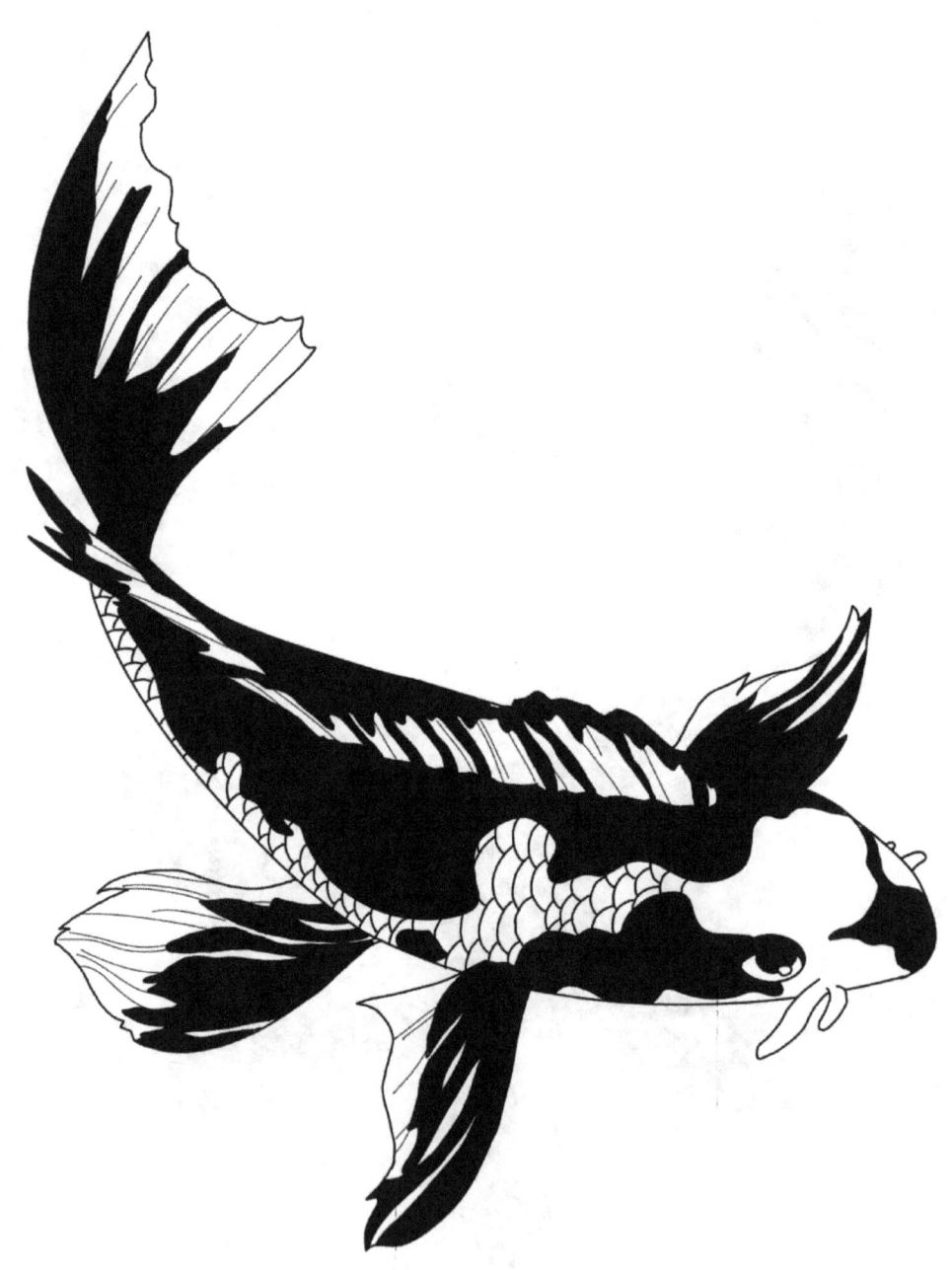

Line art version.

How to Draw A Koi 2

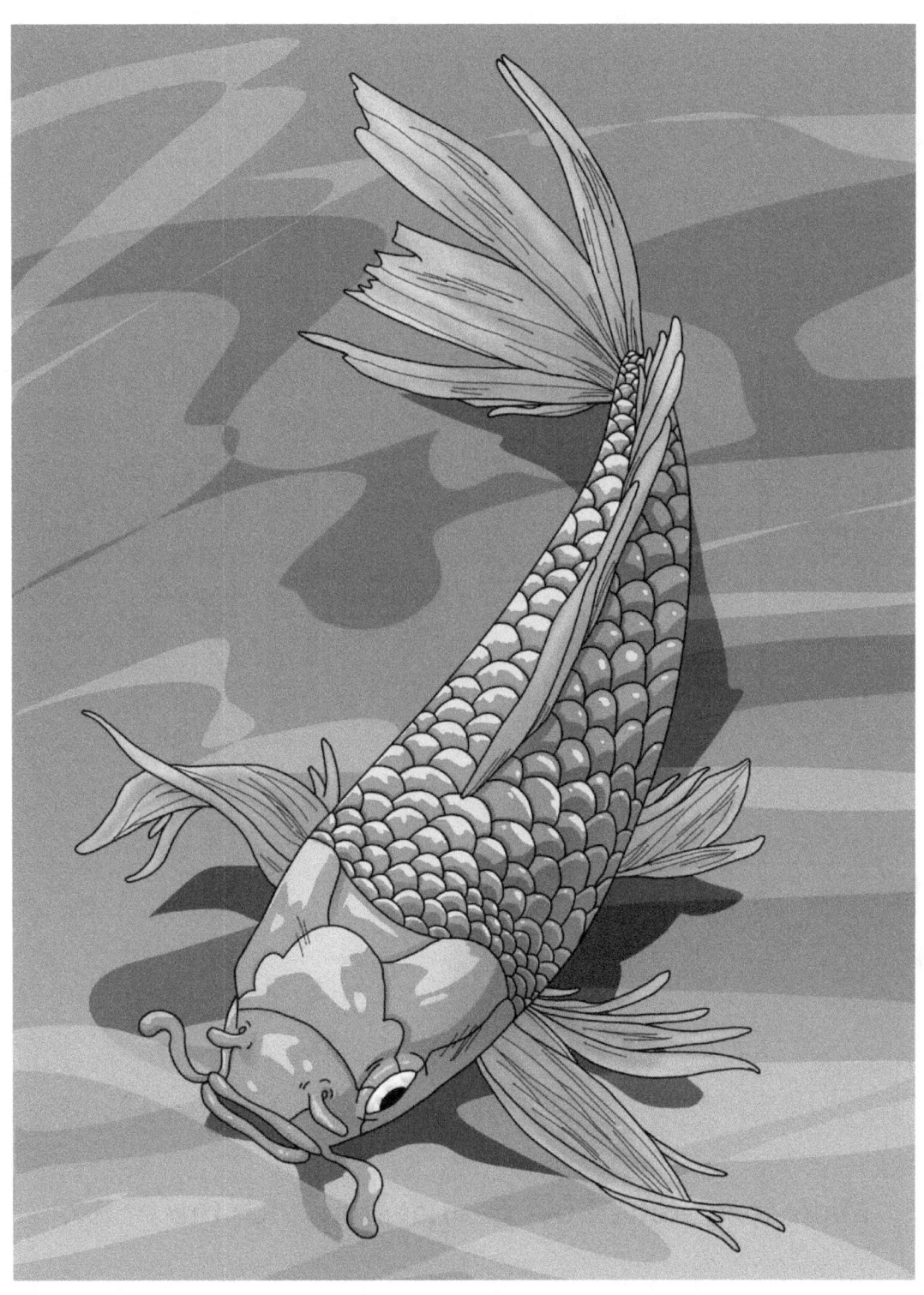

Step 1.

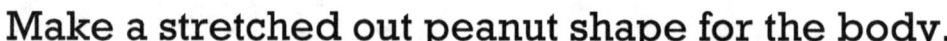

Make a stretched out peanut shape for the body.

Step 2.

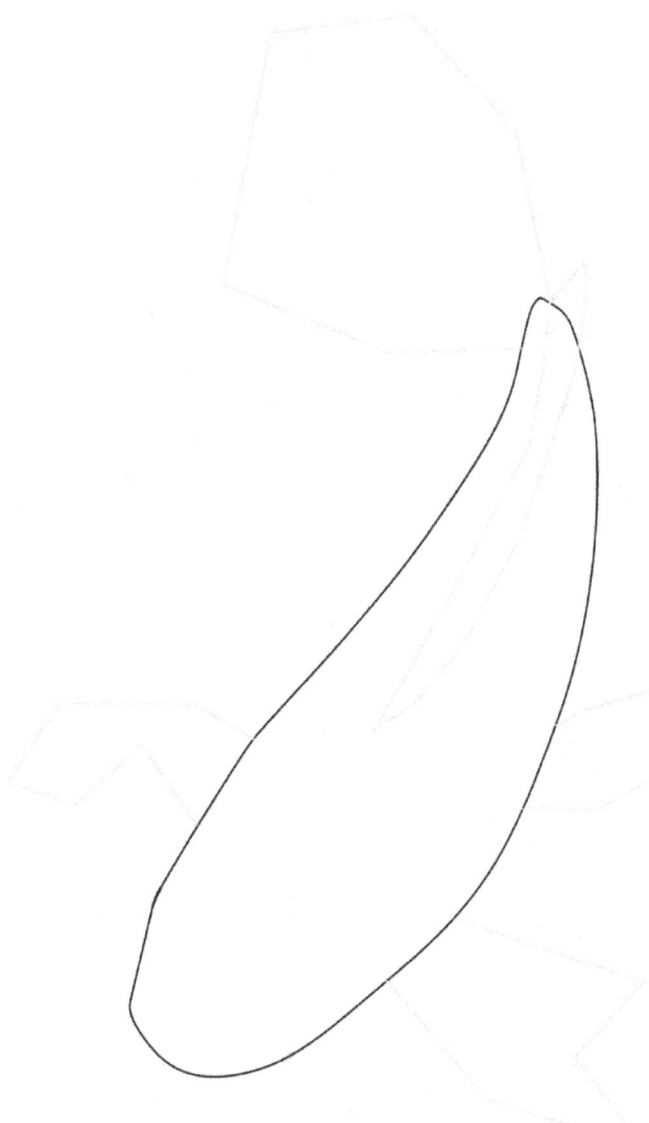

Add the outline of the dorsal fins, back fin and the tail fin as in the example.

Because of the perspective, we can only see 3 of the 4 dorsal fins.

Step 3.

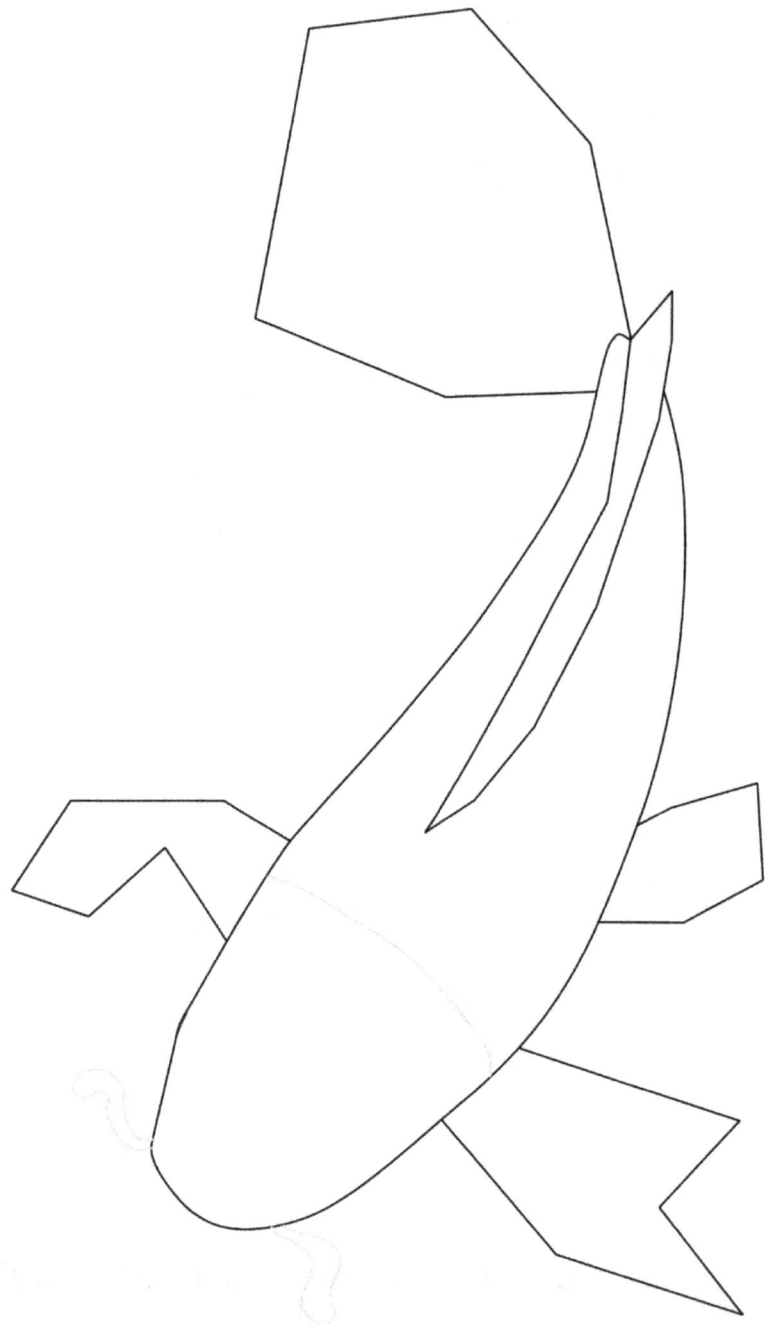

Add the appendixes to the snout and a line to separate the head
from the body.

Step 4.

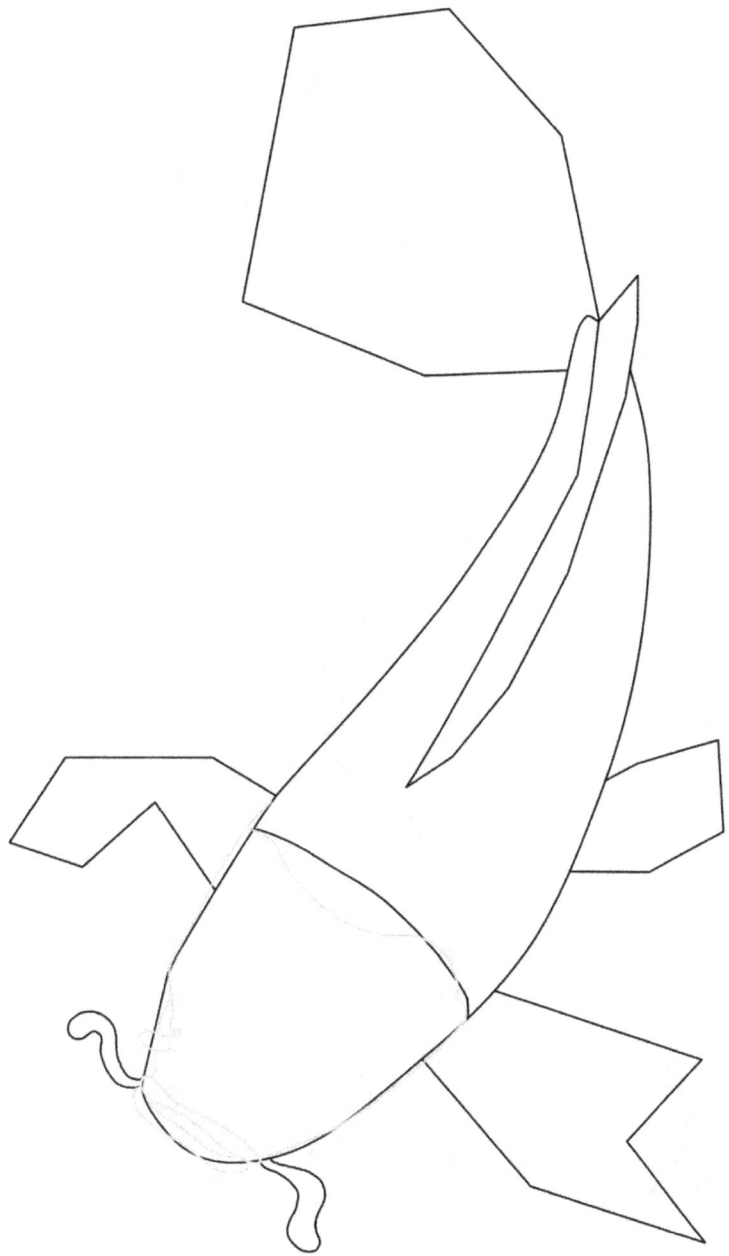

Redraw the shape of the head as in the example.

Then add some big lips to the snout and a small appendix on

the right side to follow the shape of the head.

Step 5.

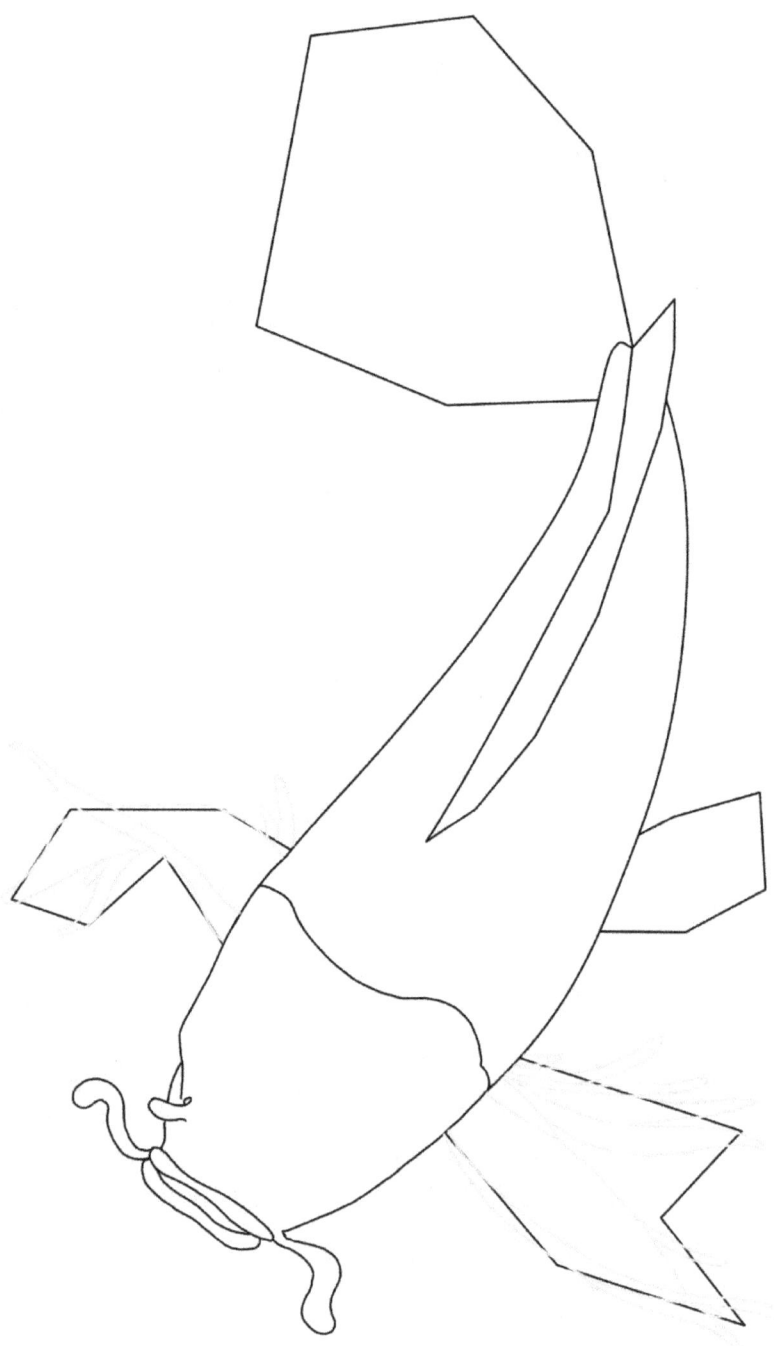

Redraw the two fins at the front. Give them swirly parts of the
fin to show the elegance of its motion.

Step 6.

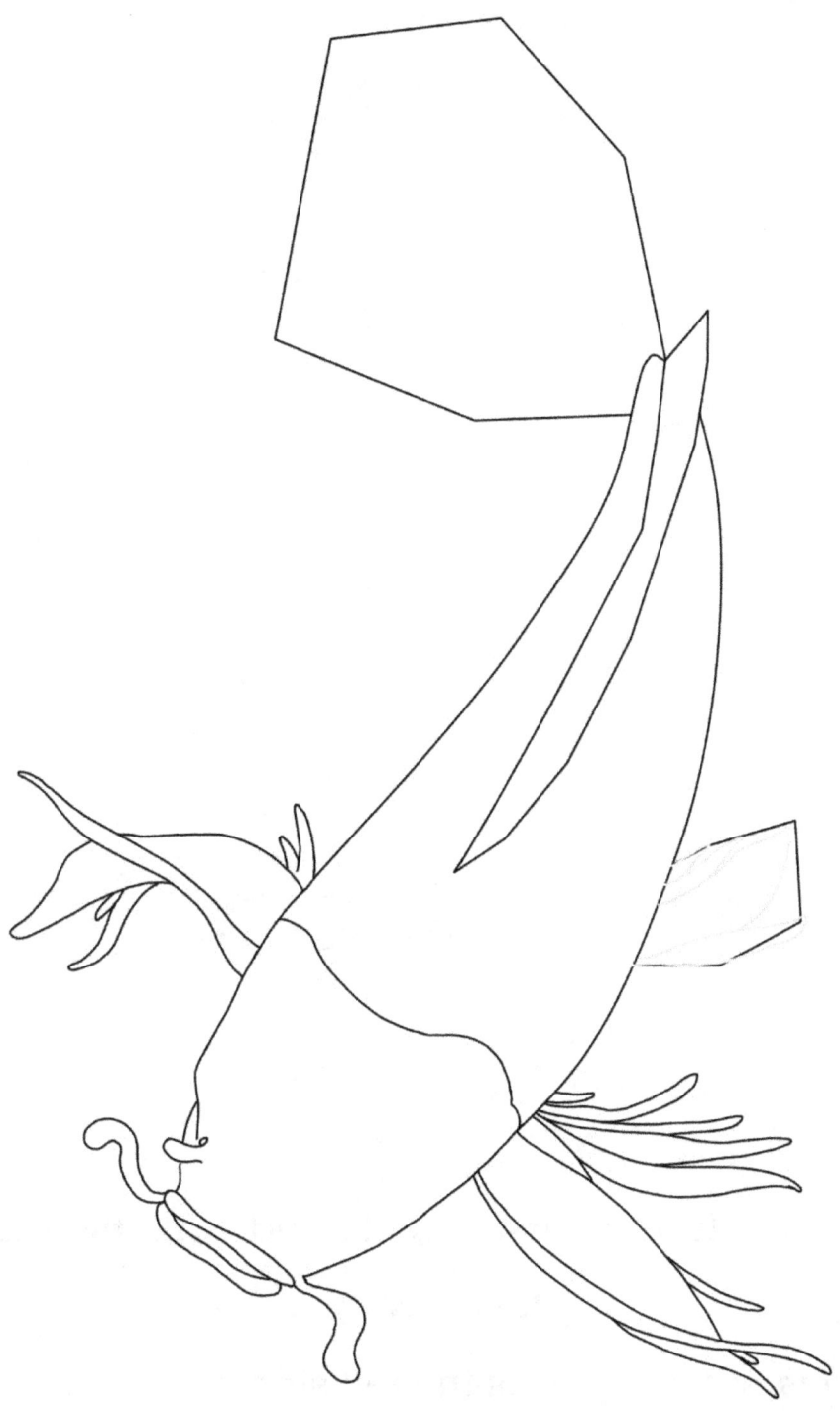

Then redraw the third fin in a similar way.

Step 7.

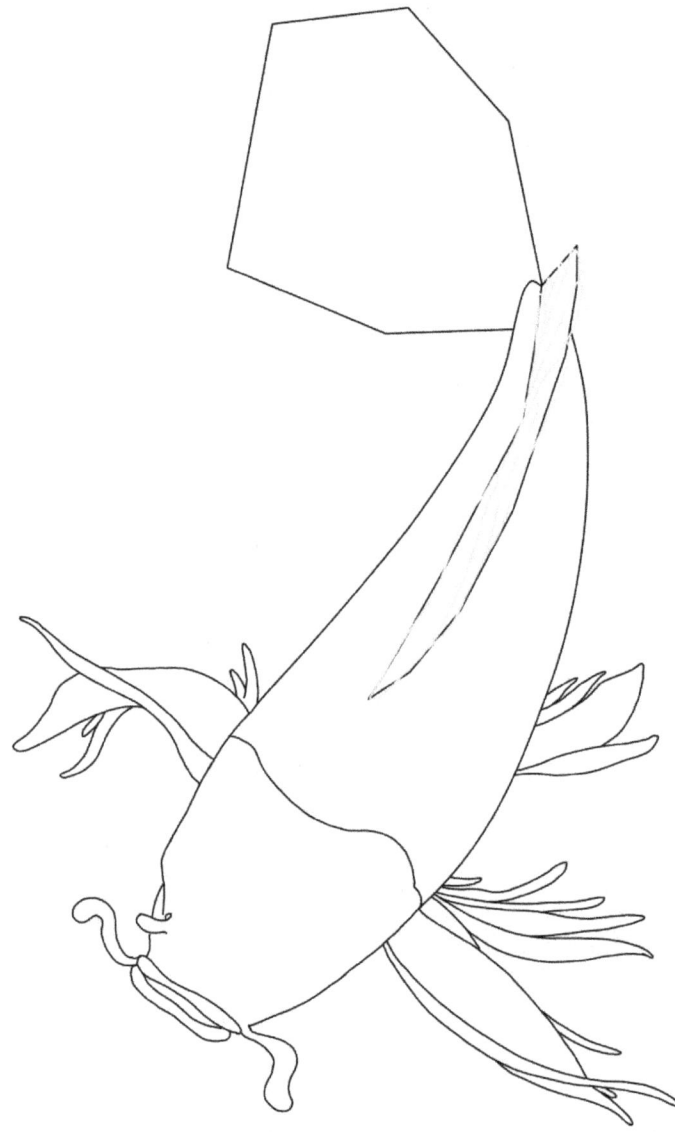

The back fin swirls in the water as it bends with the motion of the body.

Because of this, we see part of the left side in the front and that of the right side at the back.

Separate the fine by draw thicker parts in a row.

Step 8.

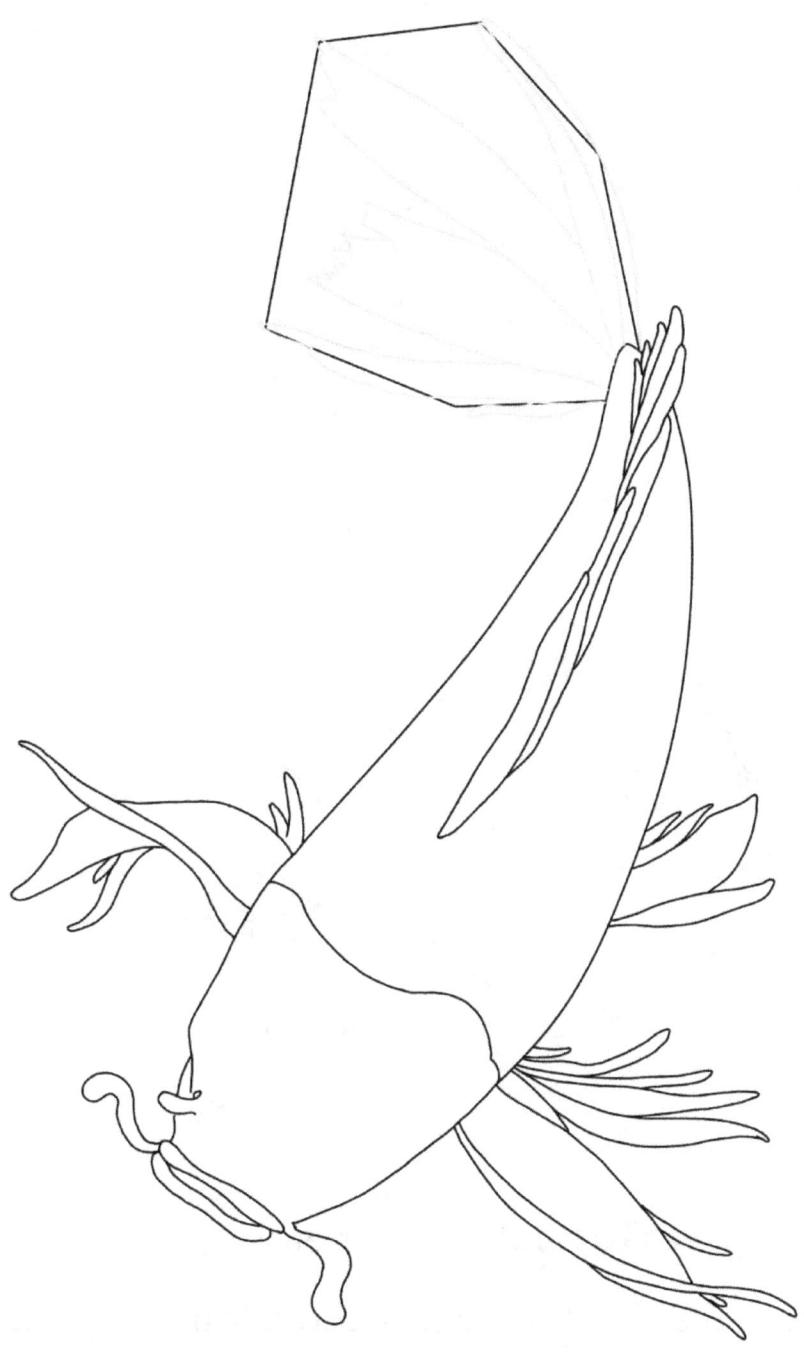

Now redraw the tail fin to make it just as elegant as the others.

Make sure to use the example to help you along.

Step 9.

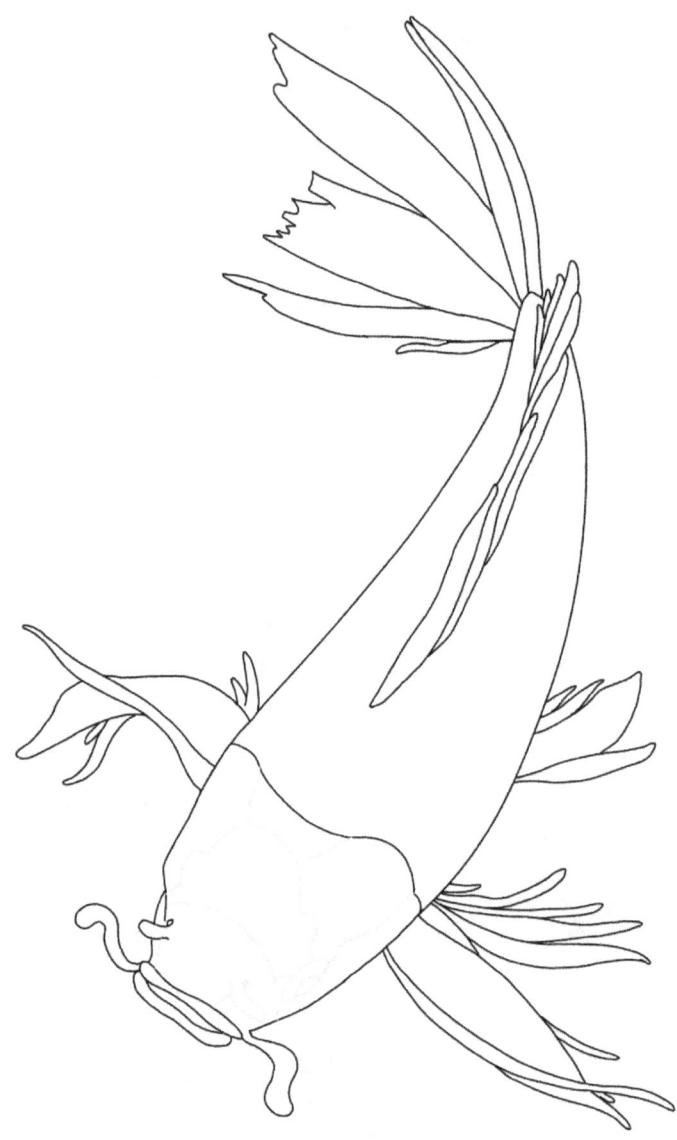

Go back to the head.

Add the eye to the side of the head and a fourth appendix right underneath it, showing where its nose hole is.

Then add the pattern to its head to separate it into different parts. See how it almost makes a unique symbol?

Step 10.

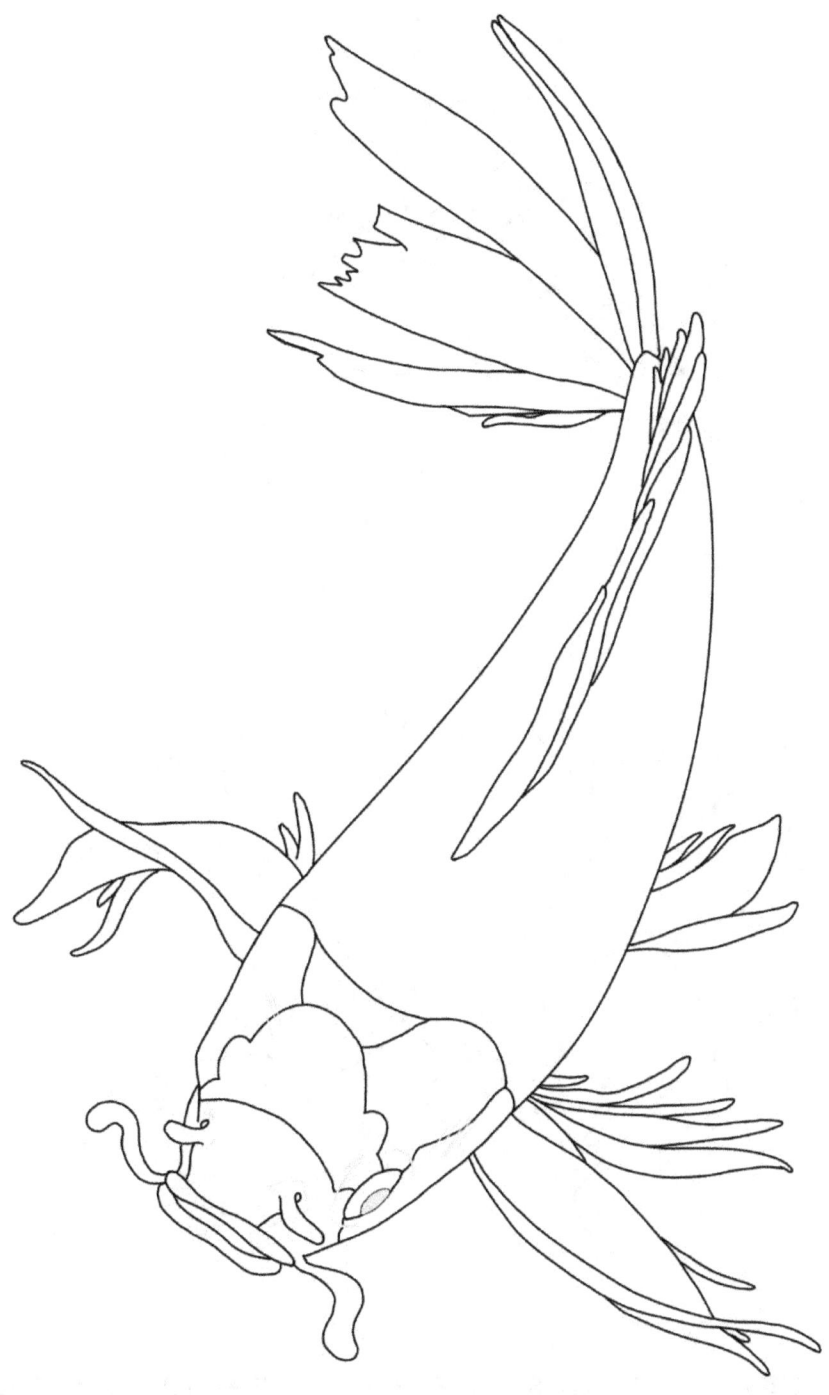

Now add some extra details to the head.

Step 11.

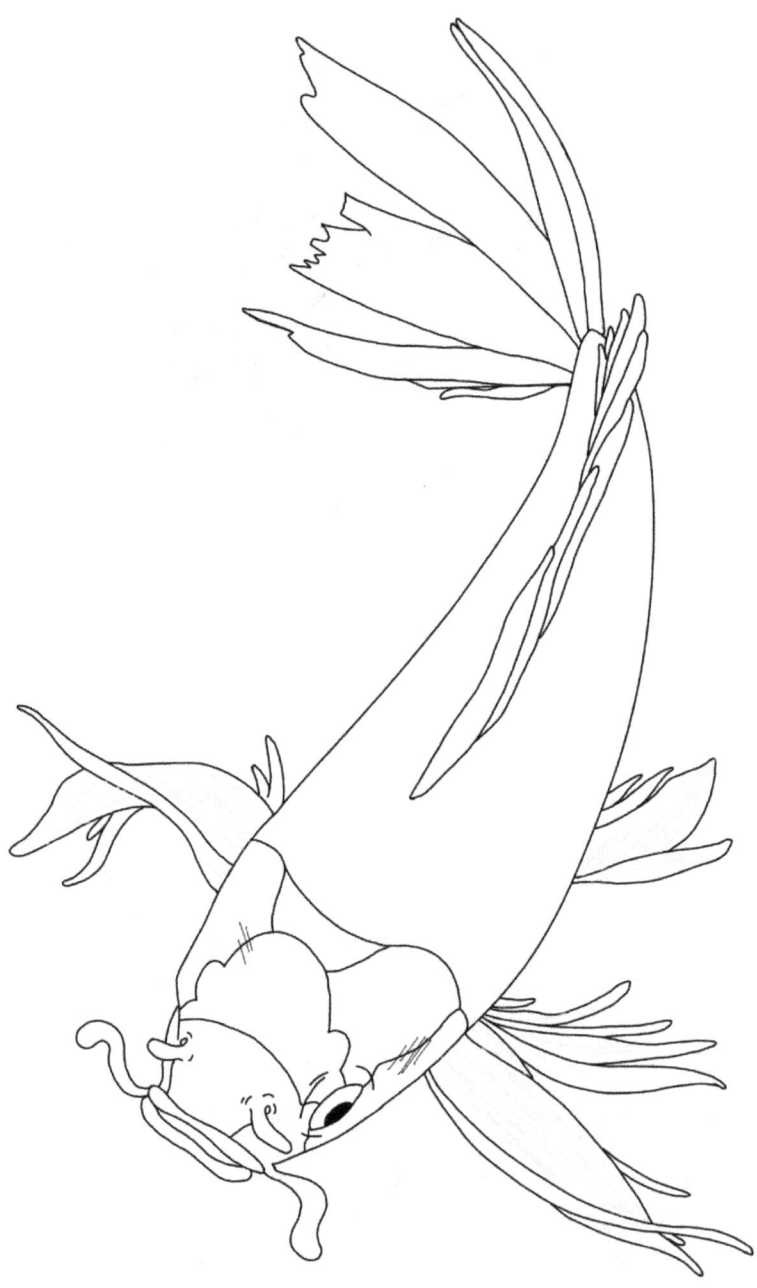

Let us continue with the fins by adding lines inside of them for

extra detail.

Start at the front.

Step 12.

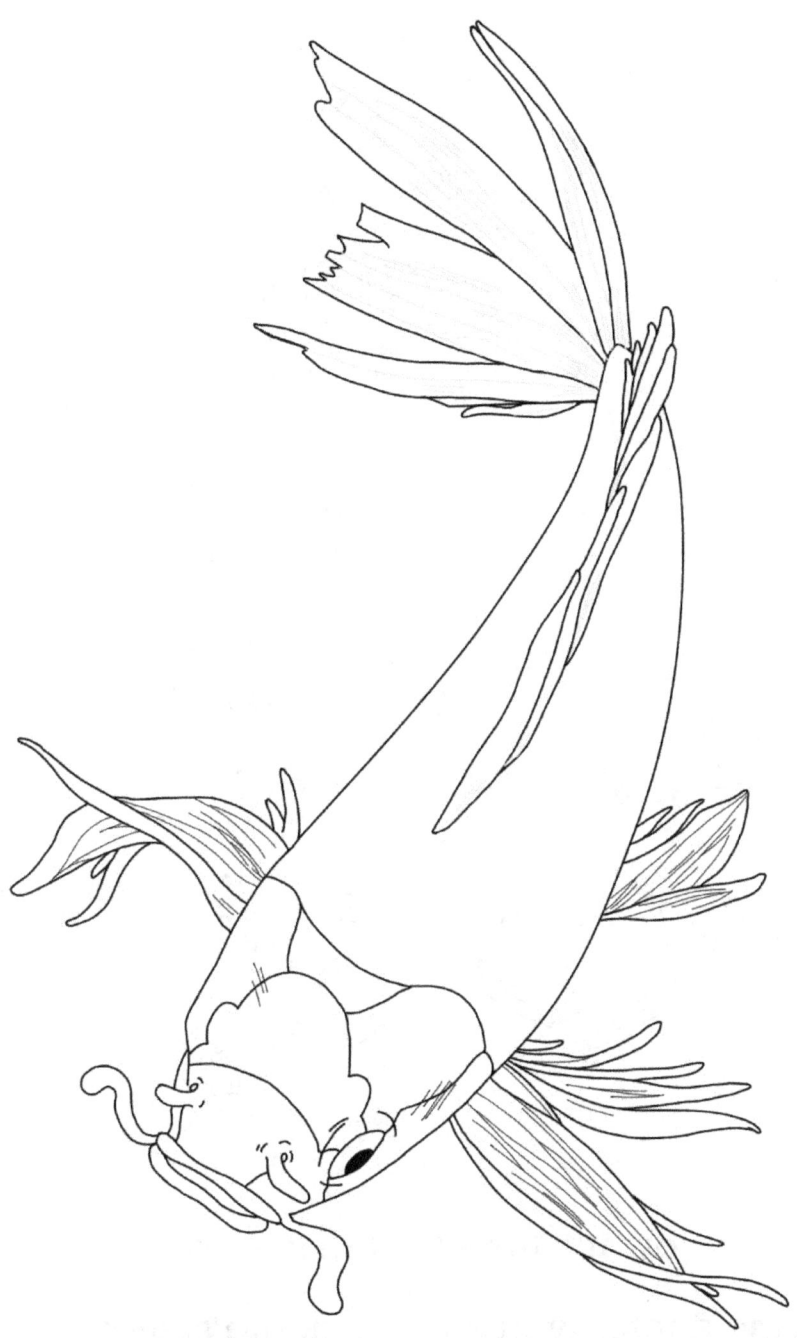

Then with the fin on the back and the tail fin. We're almost there! Doesn't it look amazing?

Step 13.

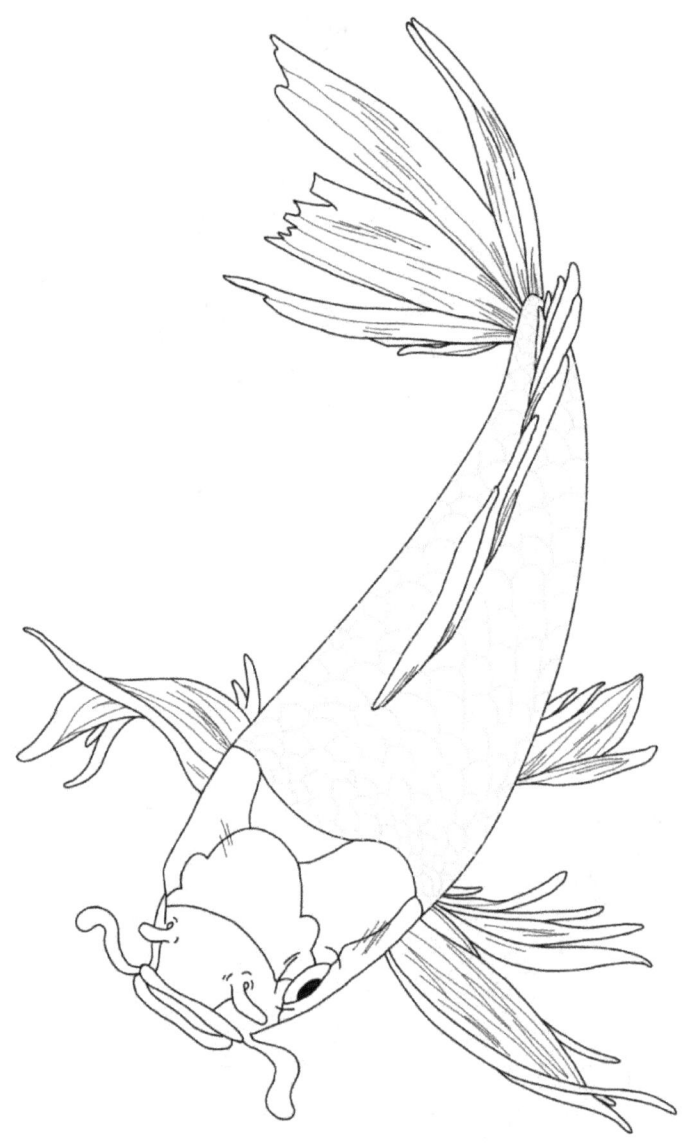

Now it's time for the scales.

Because of the anatomy of a Koi fish, the scales are almost completely on the body and not on the head.

Look at the example and start adding small C-shapes on top of each other. Make sure you follow the motion of the body.

Step 14.

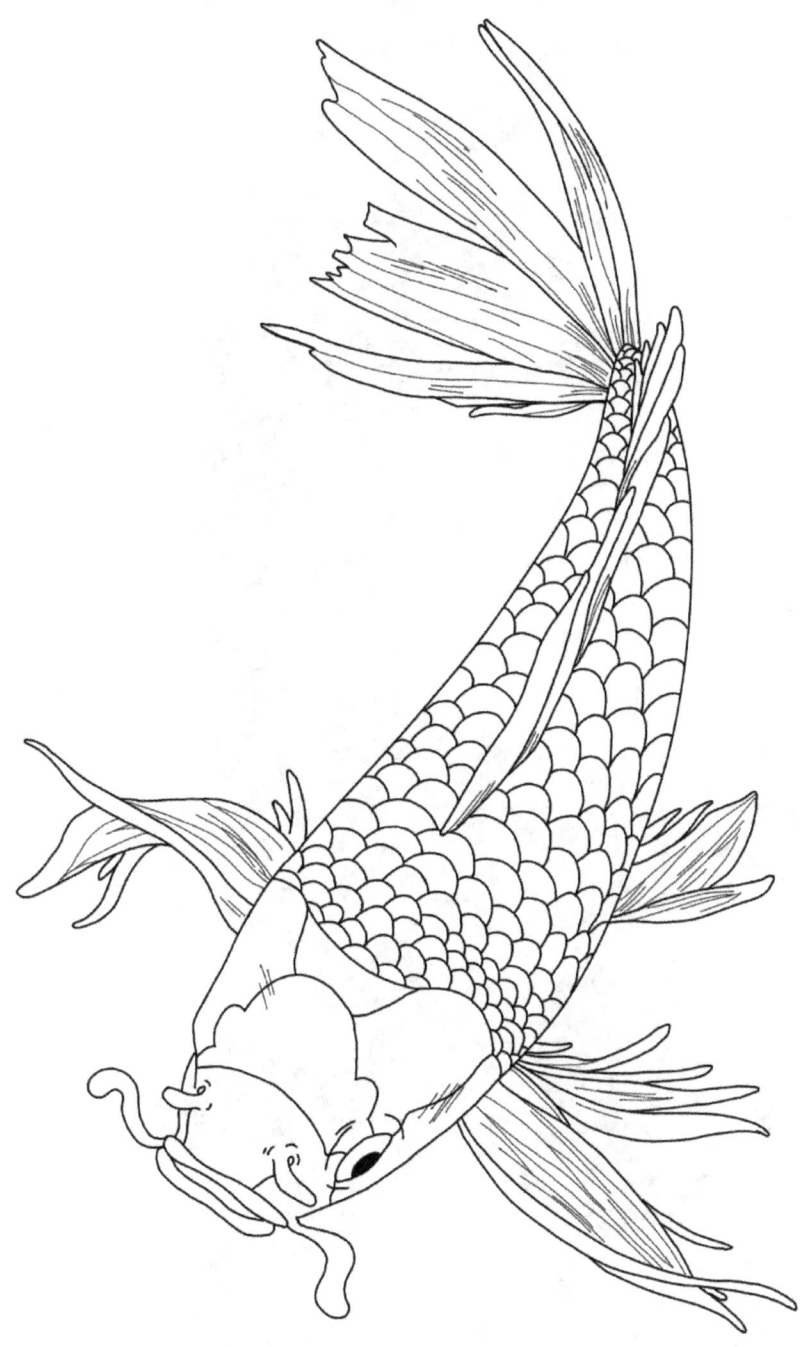

All done! It's time to color!

Step 15.

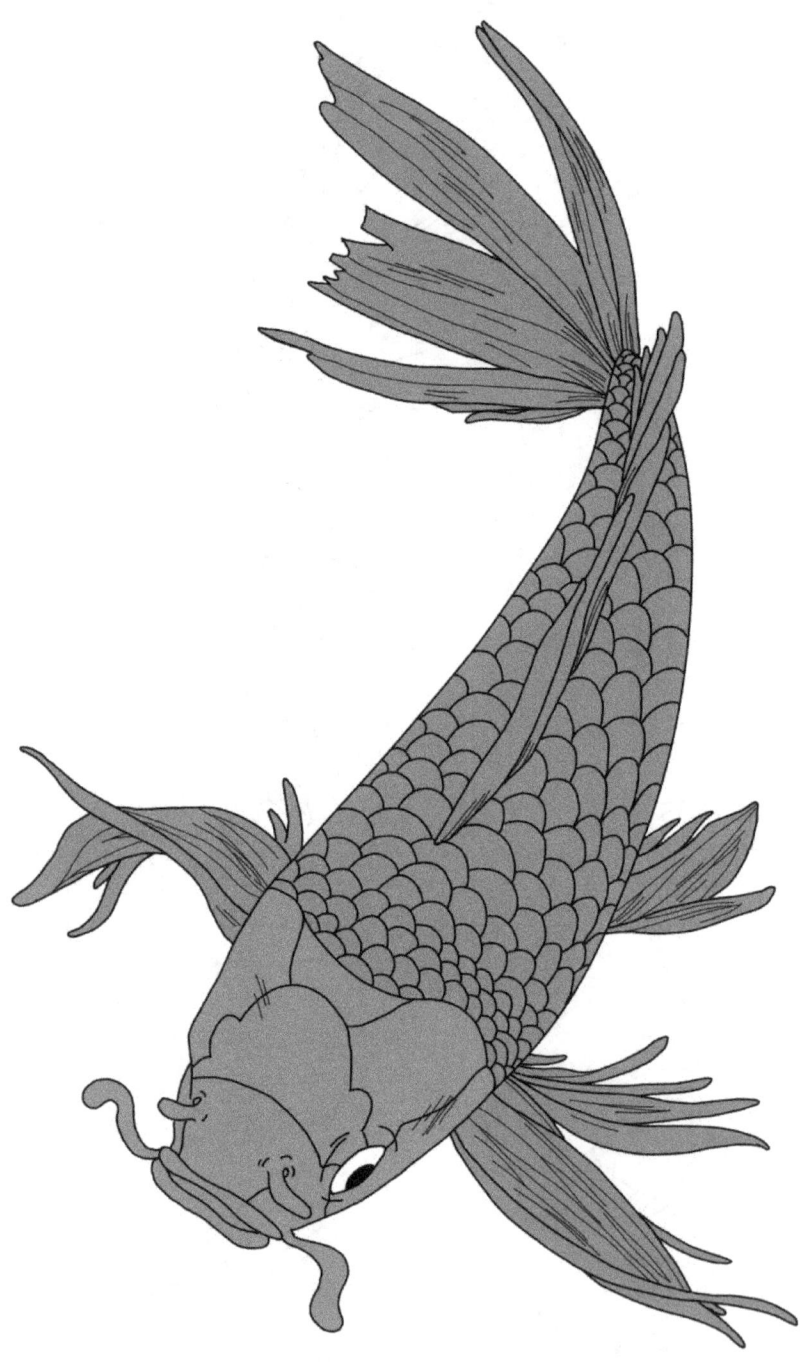

Our Koi is completely red, with a lighter red for the head.

His eye is white.

Step 16.

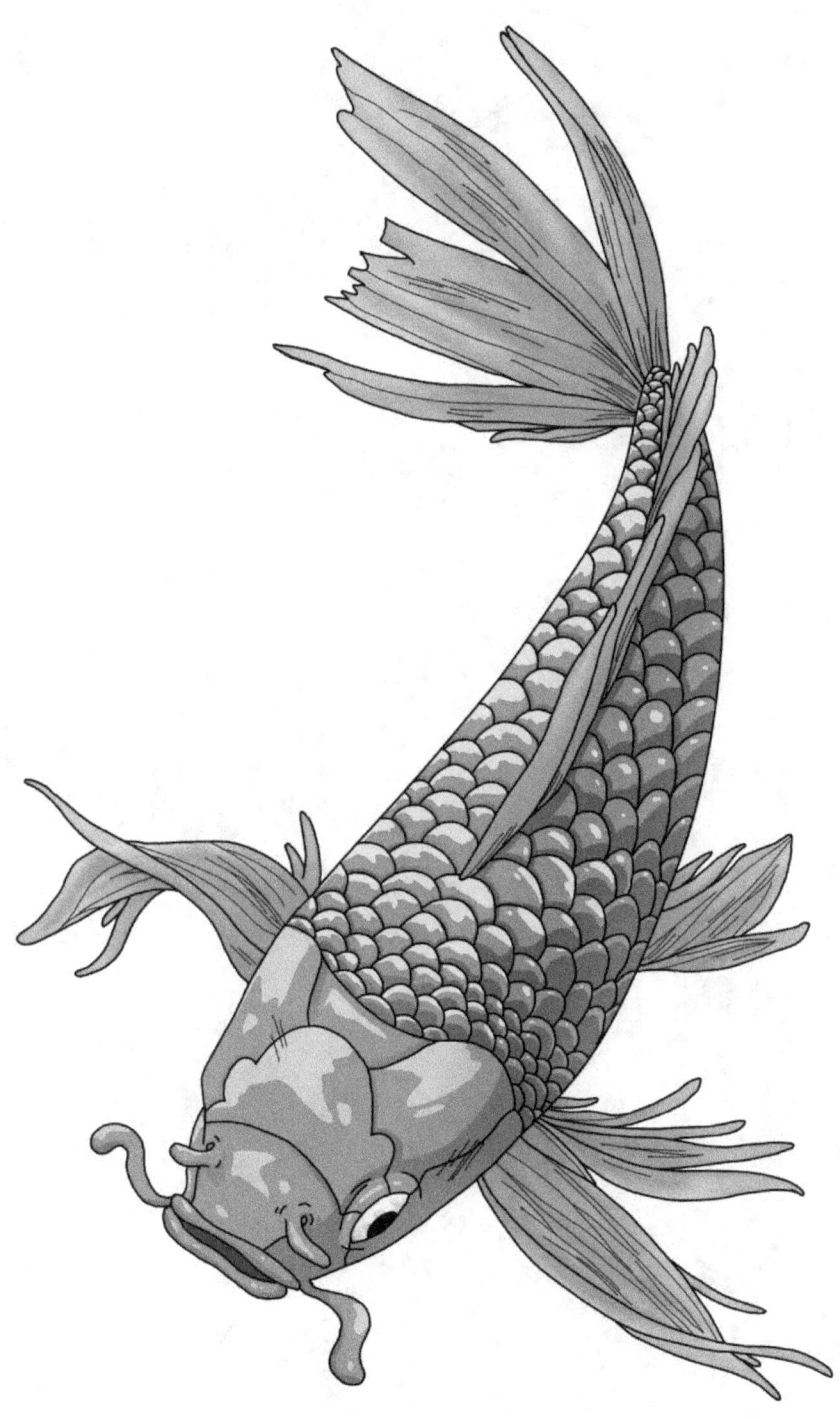

Add shadow and highlights to give our koi volume.

Step 17.

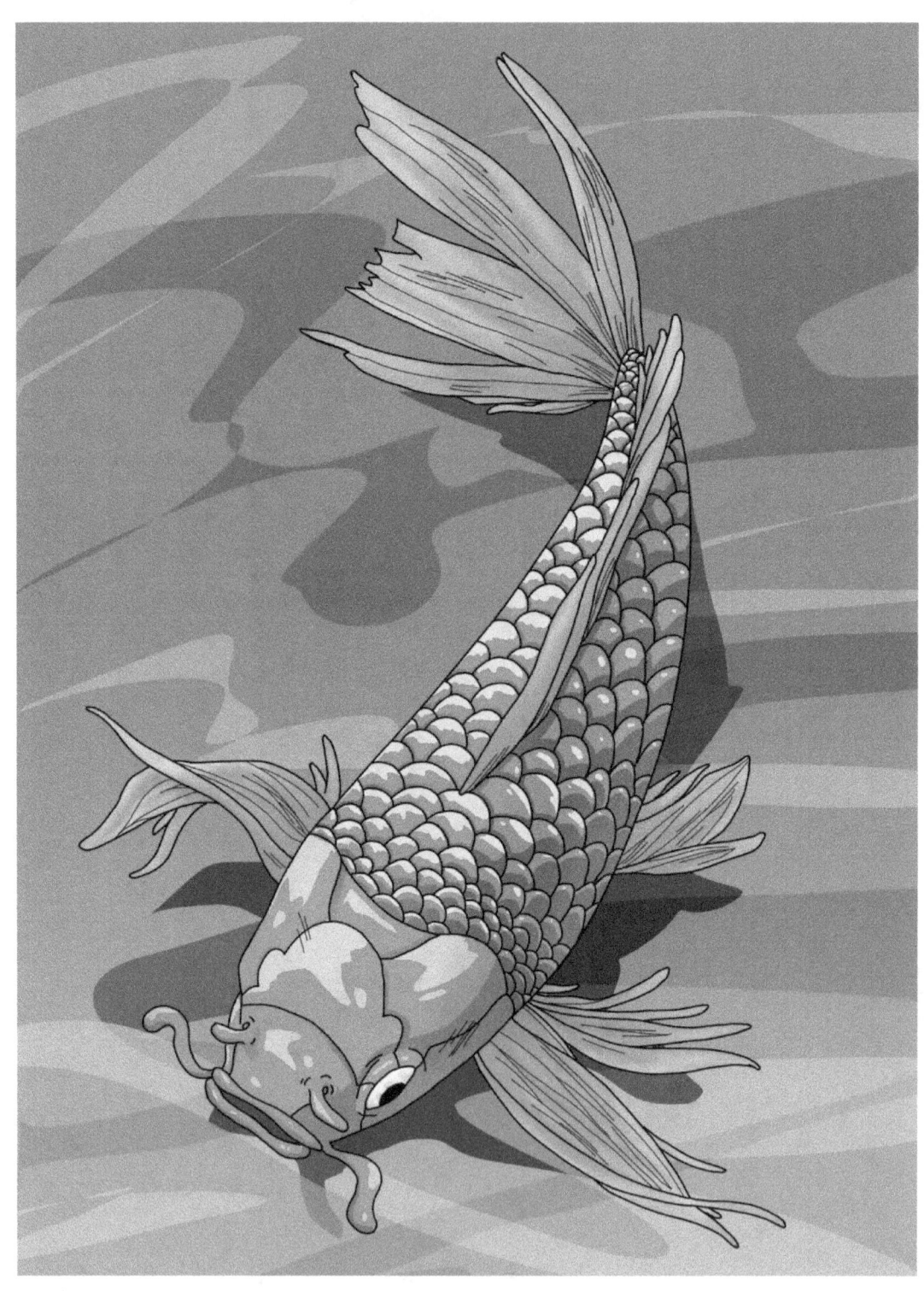

Colored version.

Step 18.

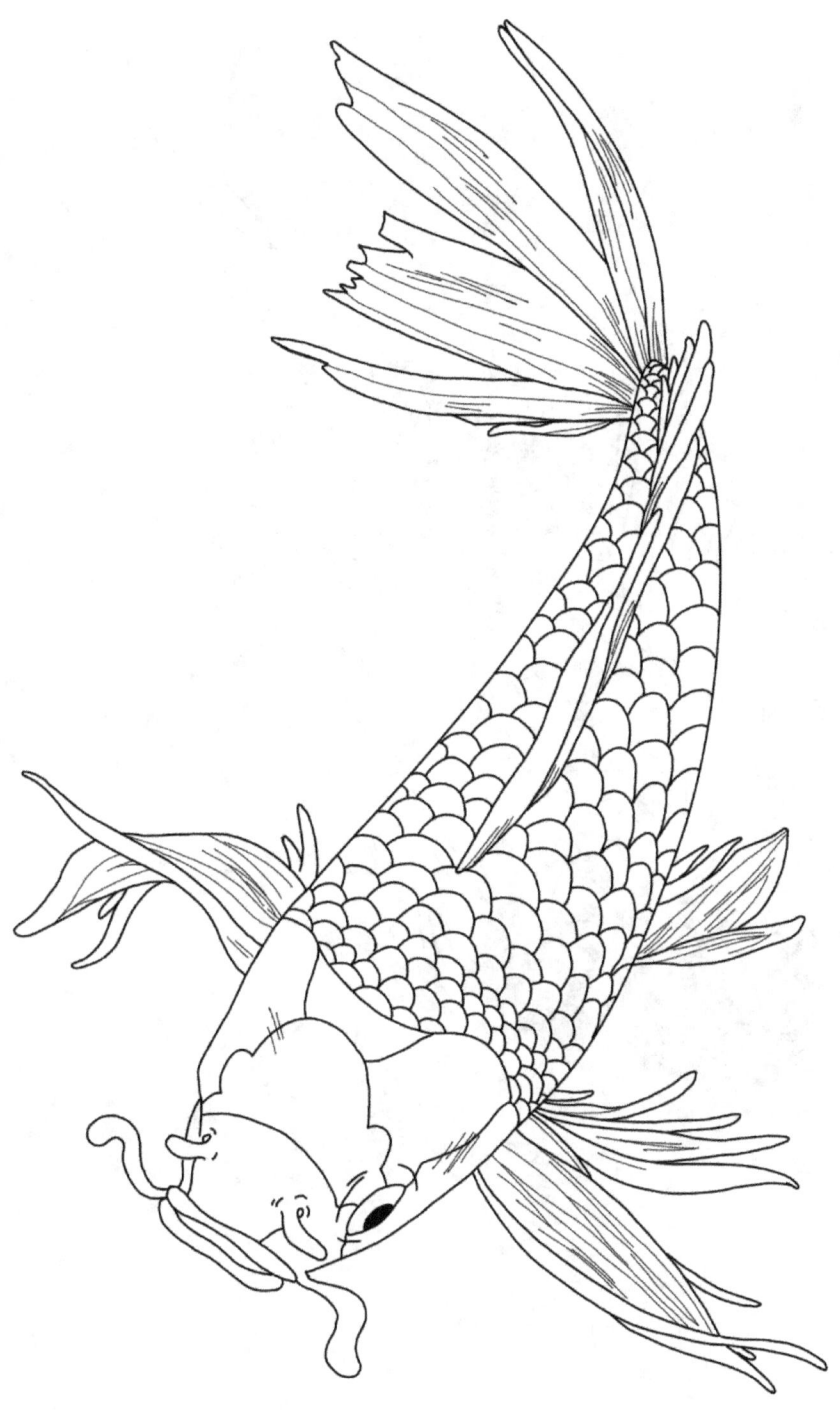

Line art version.

How to Draw A Koi 3

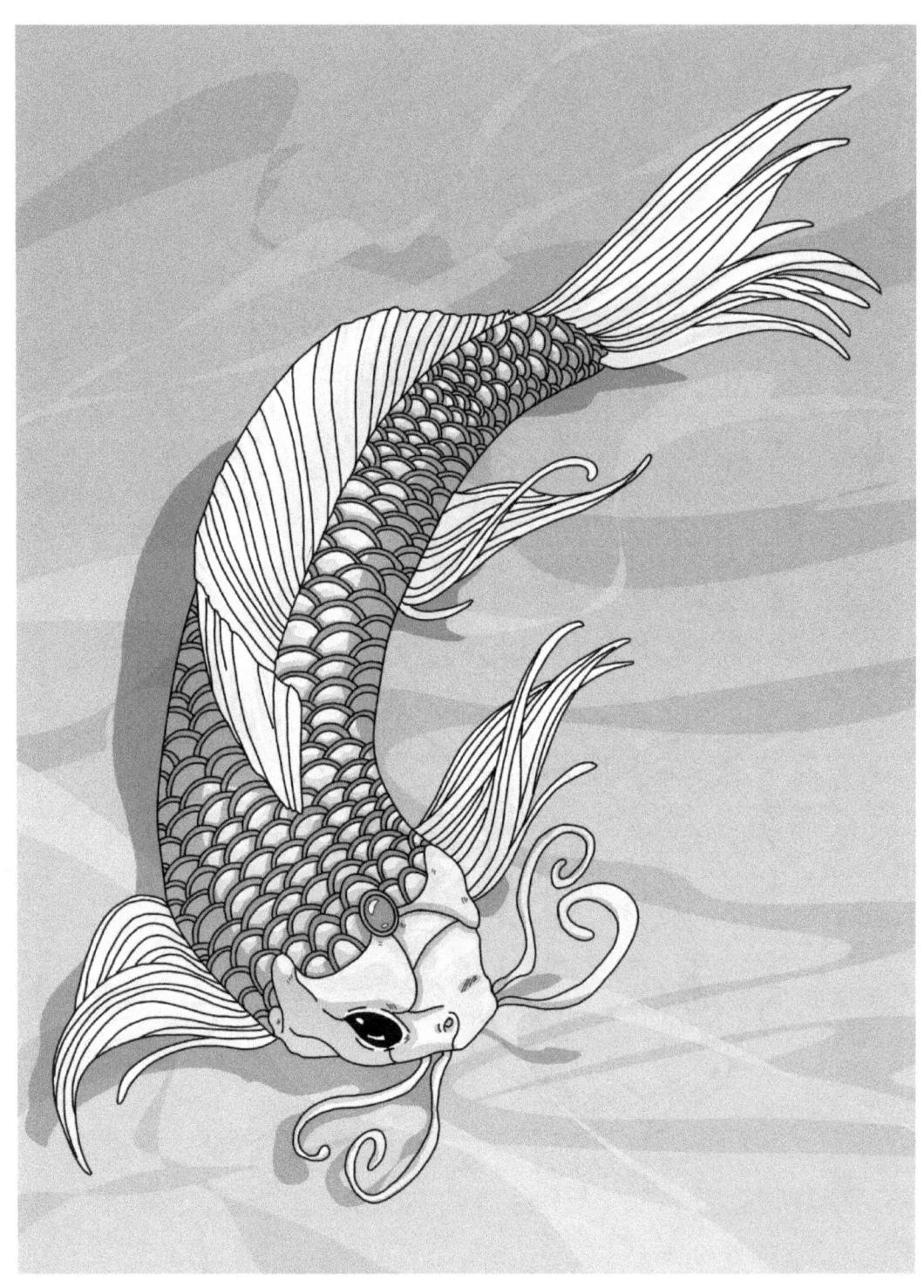

Step 1.

Make a stretched out peanut shape for the body.

Step 2.

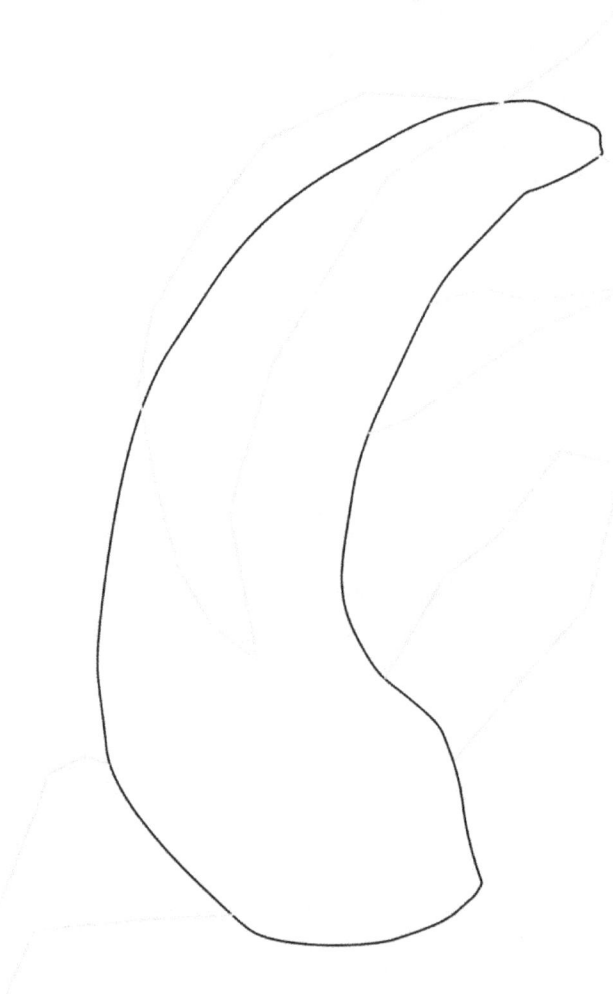

Add the outline of the dorsal fins, back fin and the tail fin as in
the example.

Because of the perspective, we can only see 3 of the 4 dorsal
fins.

Step 3.

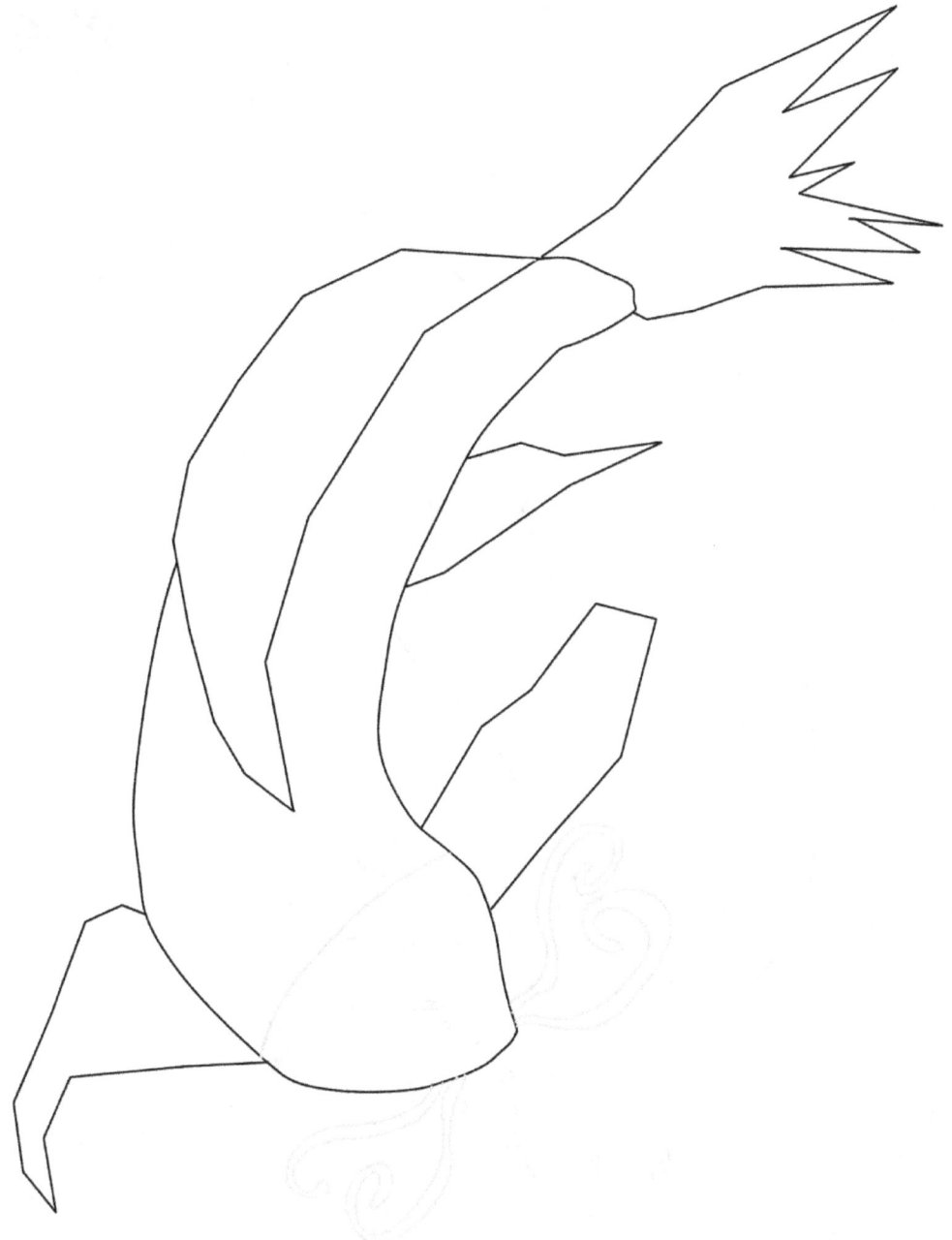

Add the appendixes to the snout and a line to separate the head

from the body.

Make sure the appendixes have an extra swirl to them.

[47]

Step 4.

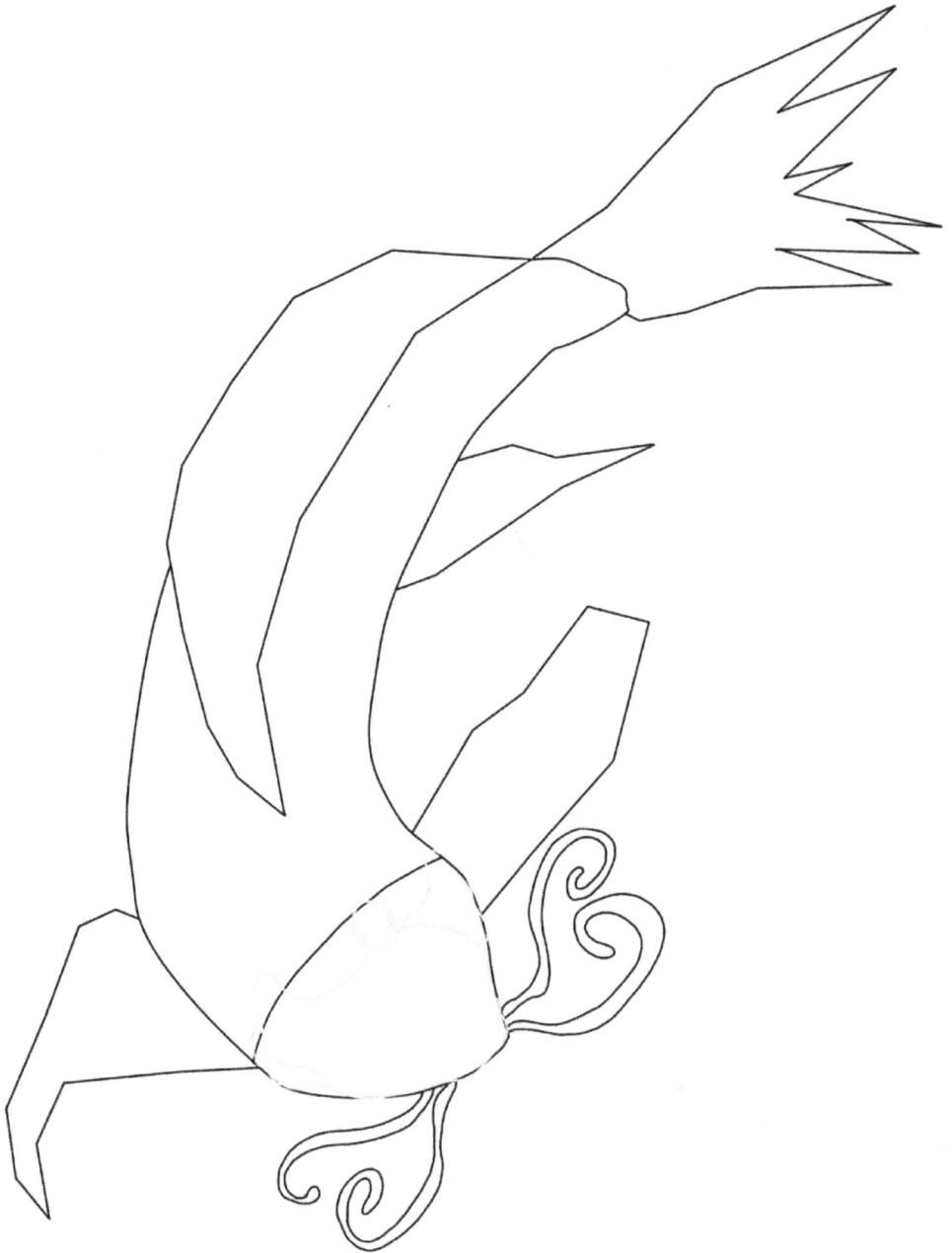

Redraw the shape of the head as in the example.

While you draw the head, give it a big circle at the top center.

This will be a jewel to decorate this enchanting koi.

Step 5.

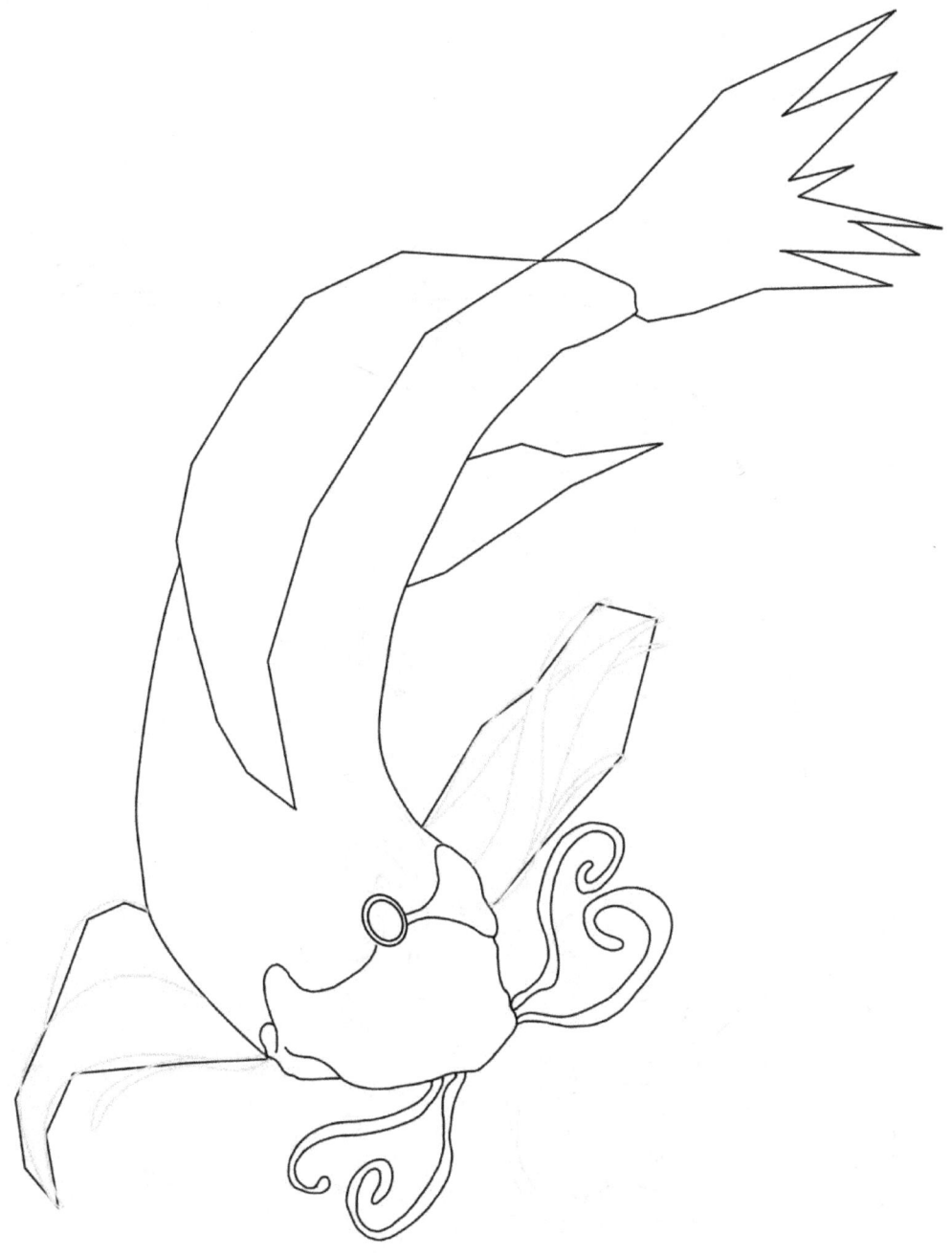

Redraw the two fins at the front. Give them swirly parts of the fin to show the elegance of its motion.

Step 6.

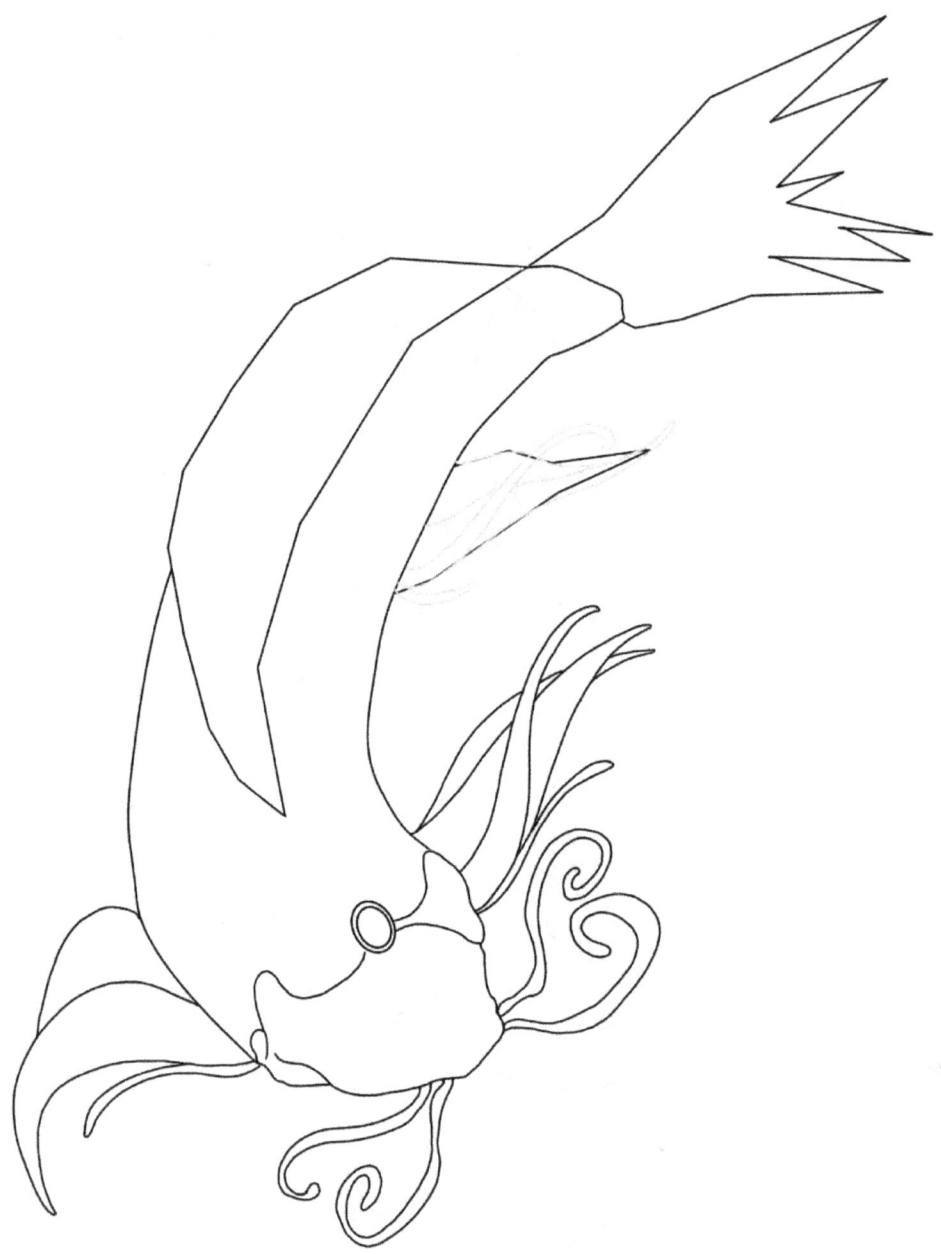

Then redraw the third fin in a similar way.

Step 7.

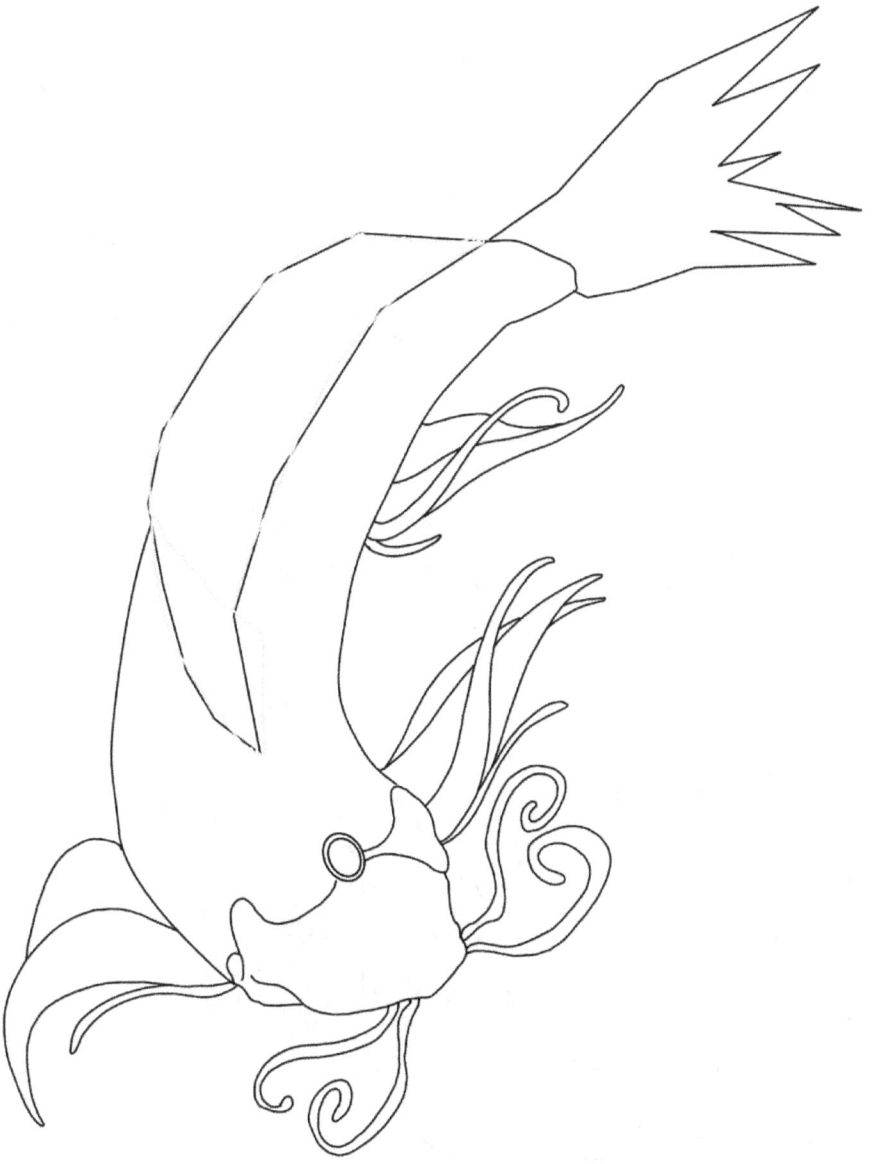

The back fin swirls in the water as it bends with the motion of
the body.

Because of this, we see part of the right side in the front and
that of the left side at the back.

Separate the fine by draw thicker parts in a row.

Step 8.

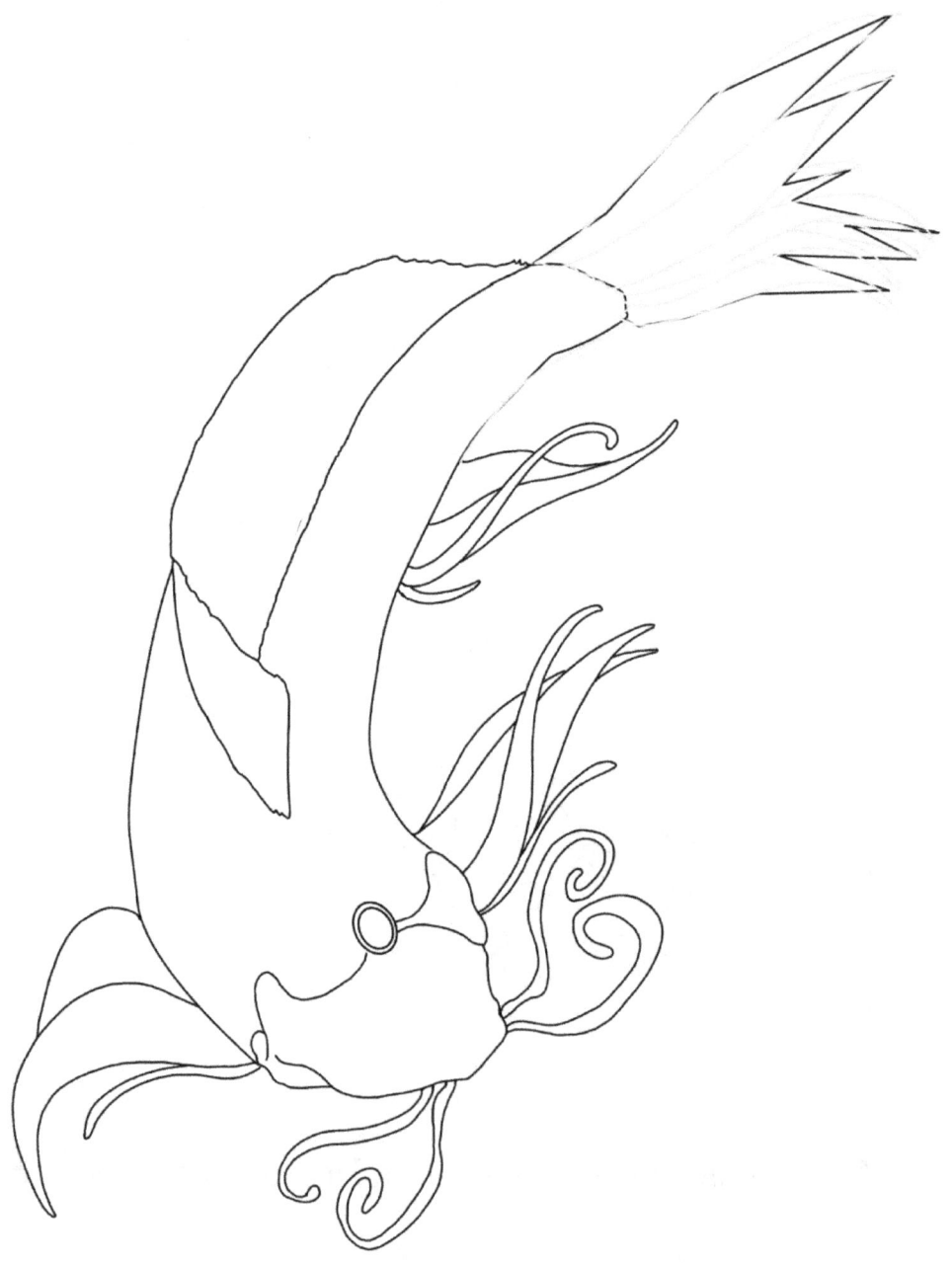

Now redraw the tail fin to make it just as elegant as the others.

Make sure to use the example to help you along.

Step 9.

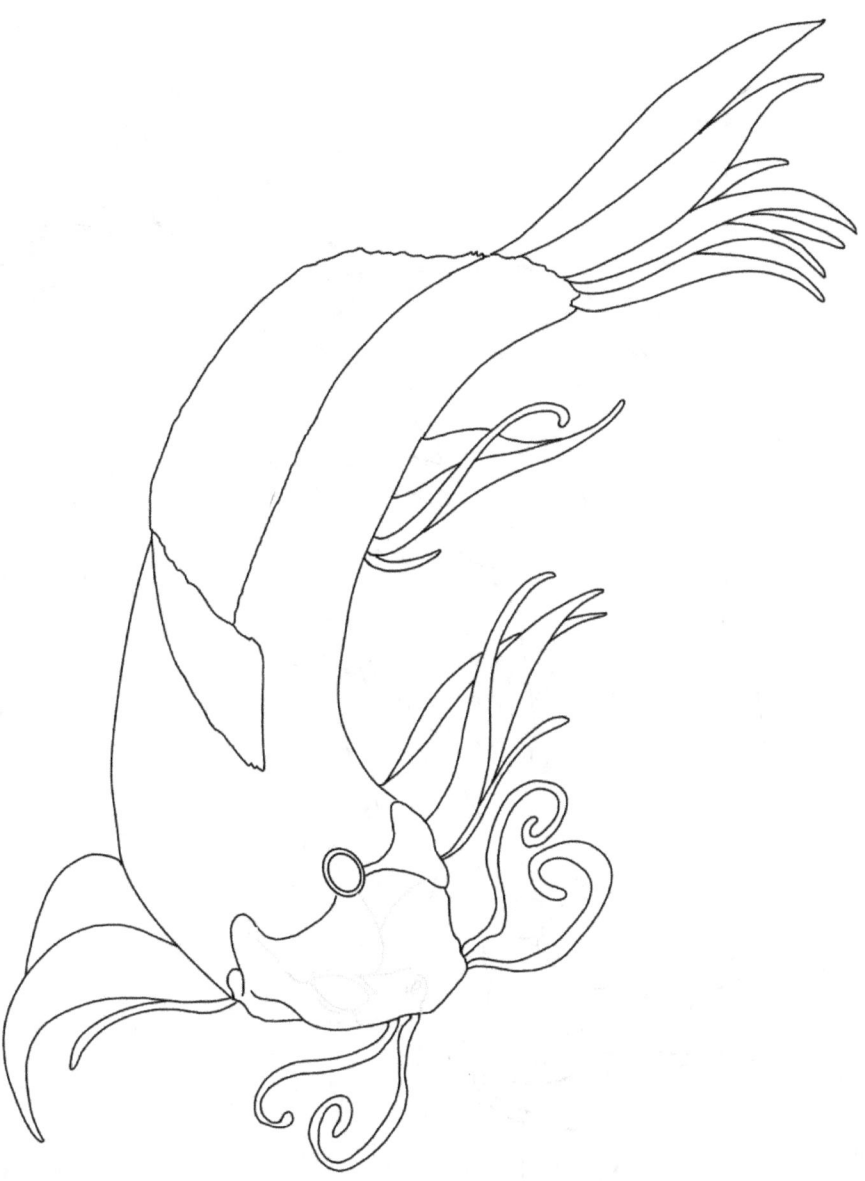

Go back to the head.

Add the eye to the side of the head add a small hole showing where its nose hole is.

Then add the pattern to its head to separate it into different parts. See how it almost makes a unique symbol?

Step 10.

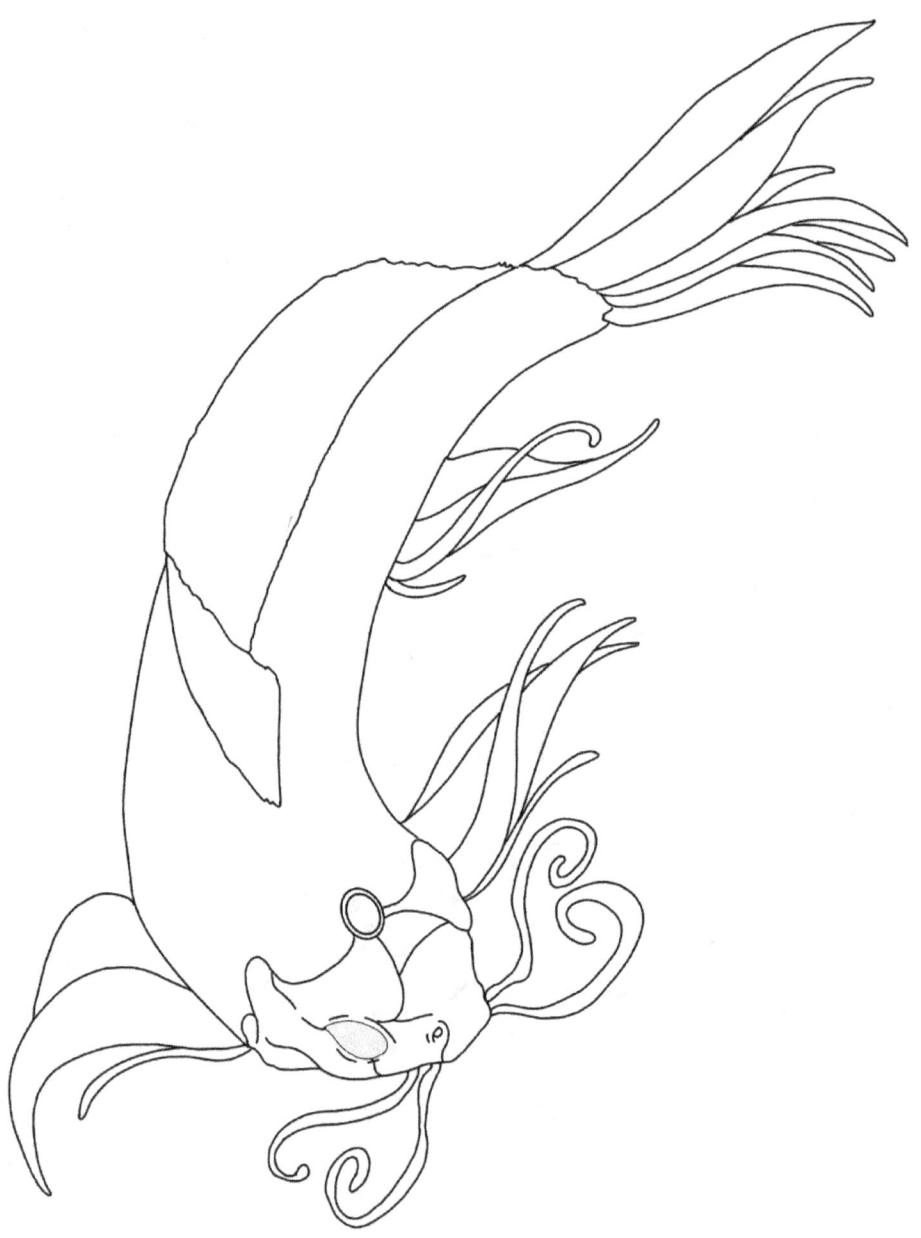

Now add some extra details to the head and color the eye
black. Leave some white for the highlights.

Then add some circular shapes inside the jewel for its
highlights.

Step 11.

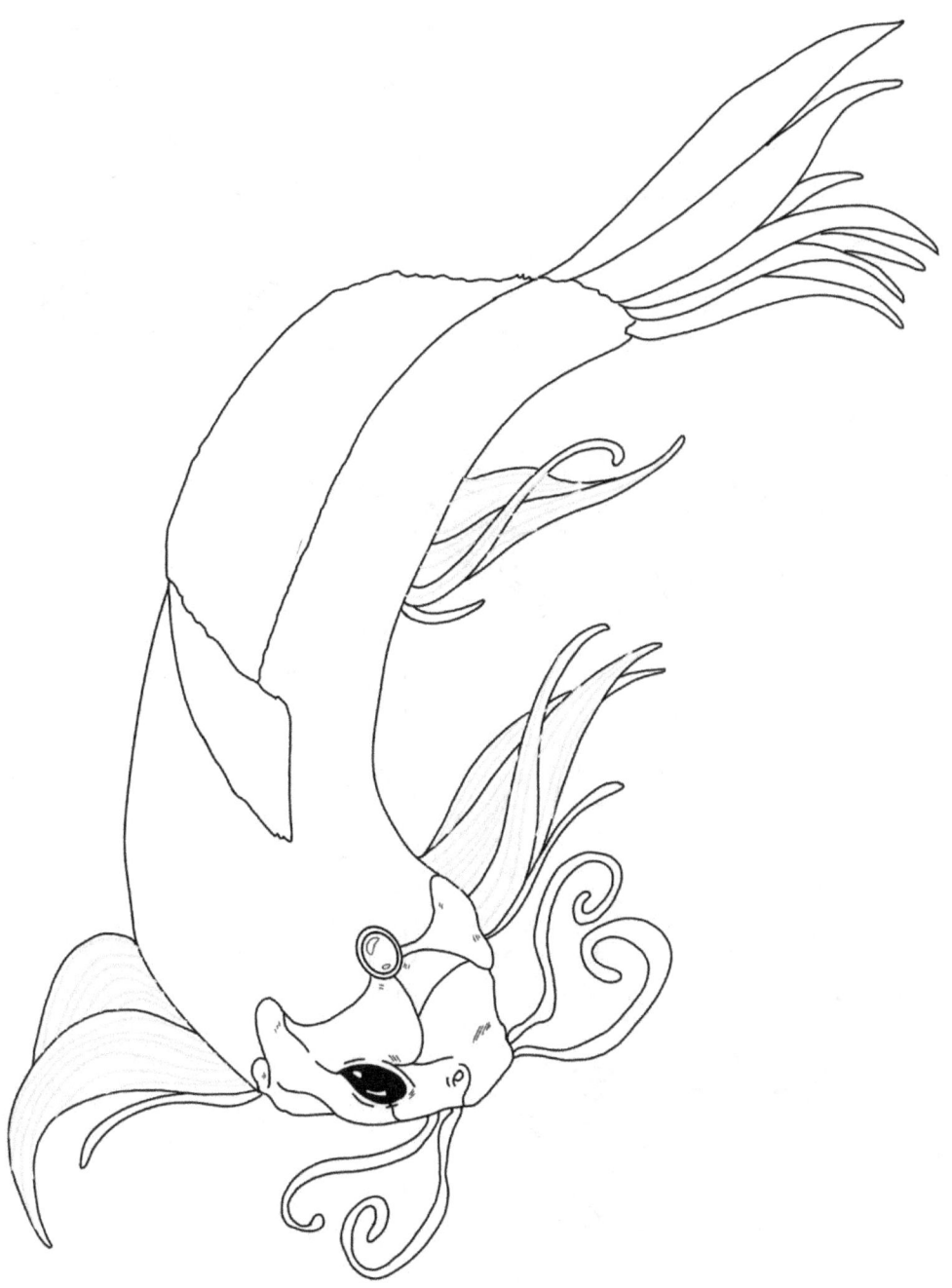

Let us continue with the fins by adding lines inside of them for

extra detail.

Start at the front.

Step 12.

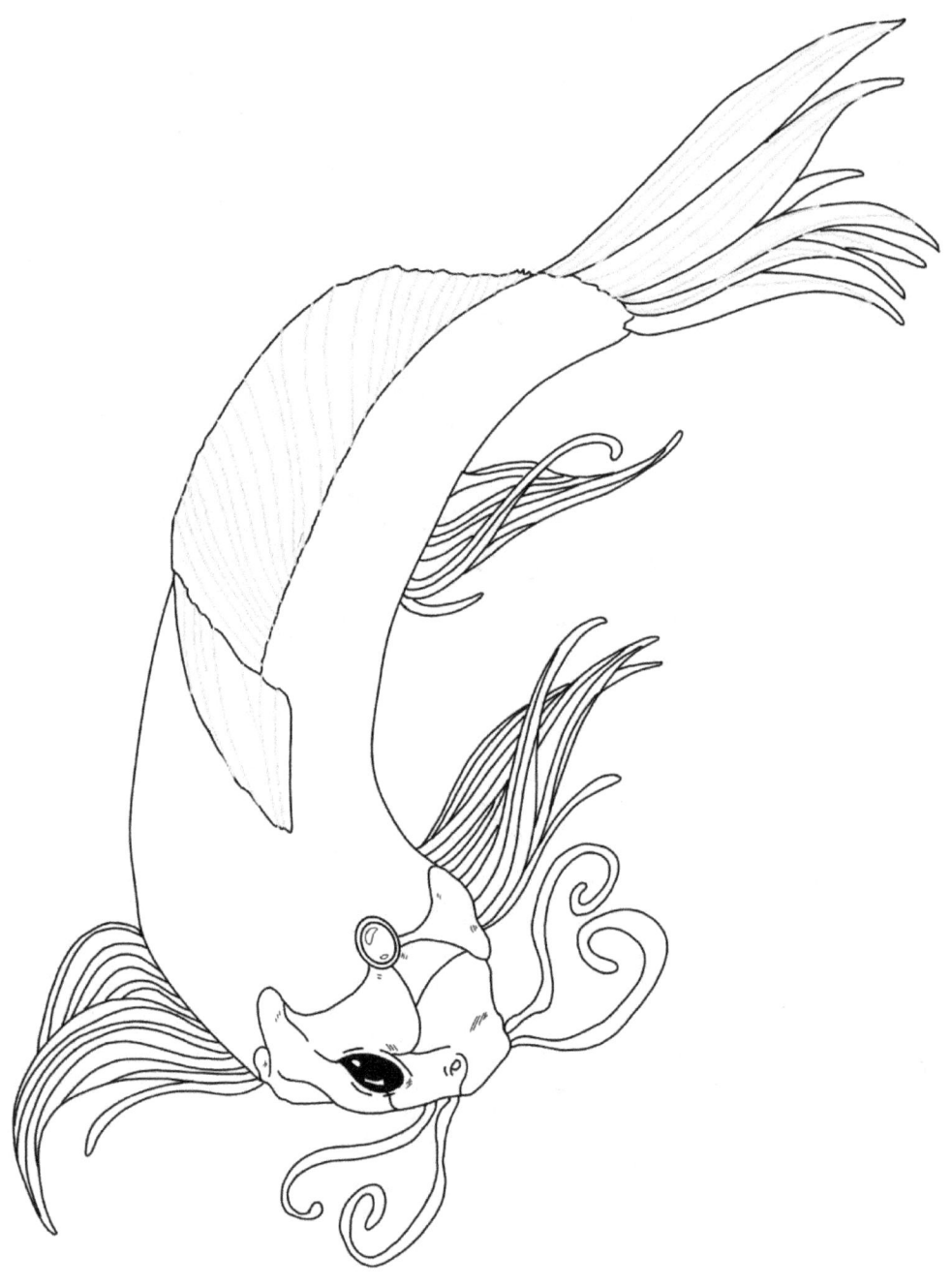

Then with the fin on the back and the tail fin. We're almost there! Doesn't it look amazing?

Step 13.

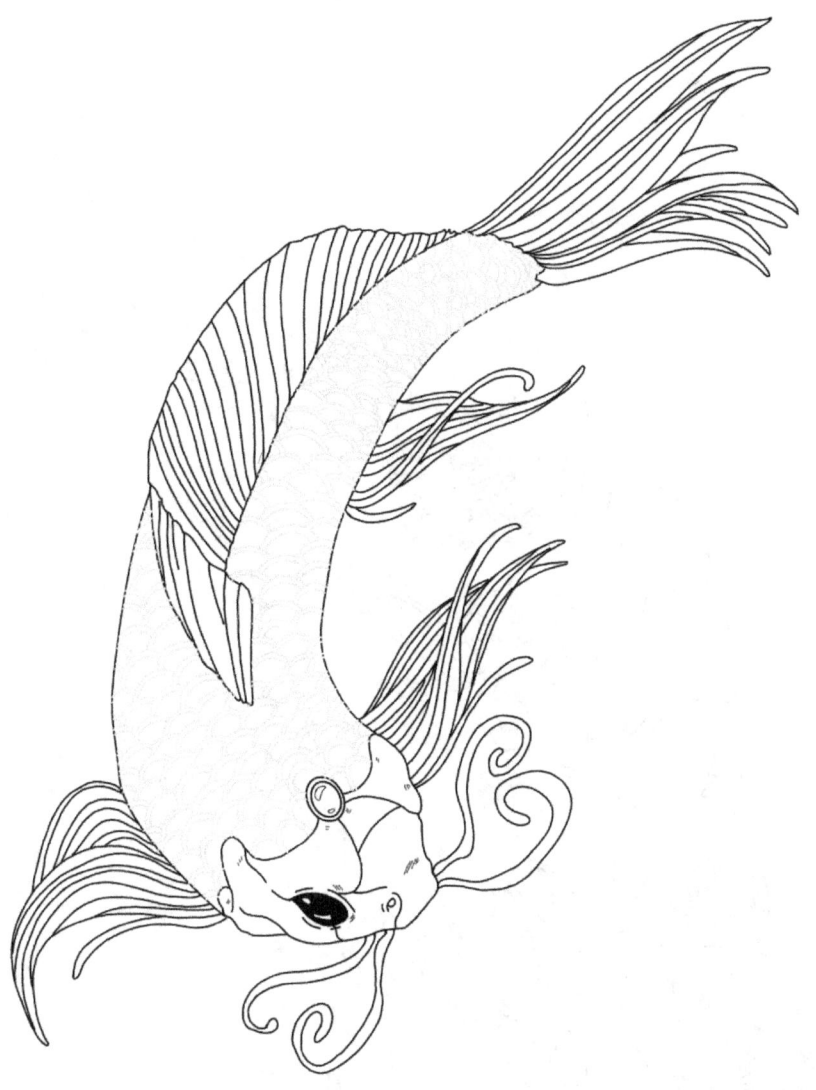

Now it's time for the scales.

Because of the anatomy of a Koi fish, the scales are almost completely on the body and not on the head.

Look at the example and start adding small C-shapes on top of each other. Make sure you follow the motion of the body. Then add another smaller C-shape inside the scales for extra effect.

Step 14.

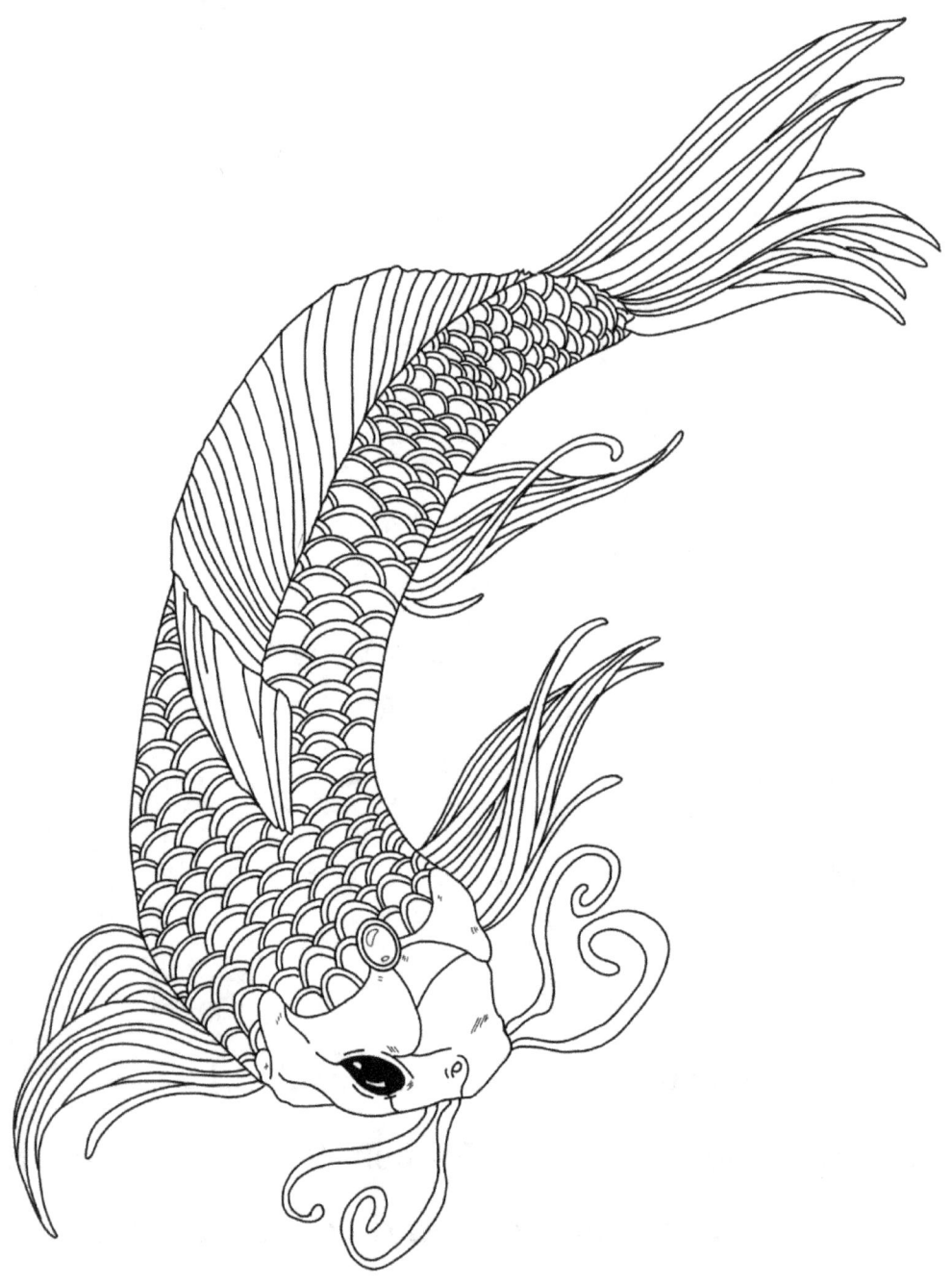

All done! It's time to color!

Step 15.

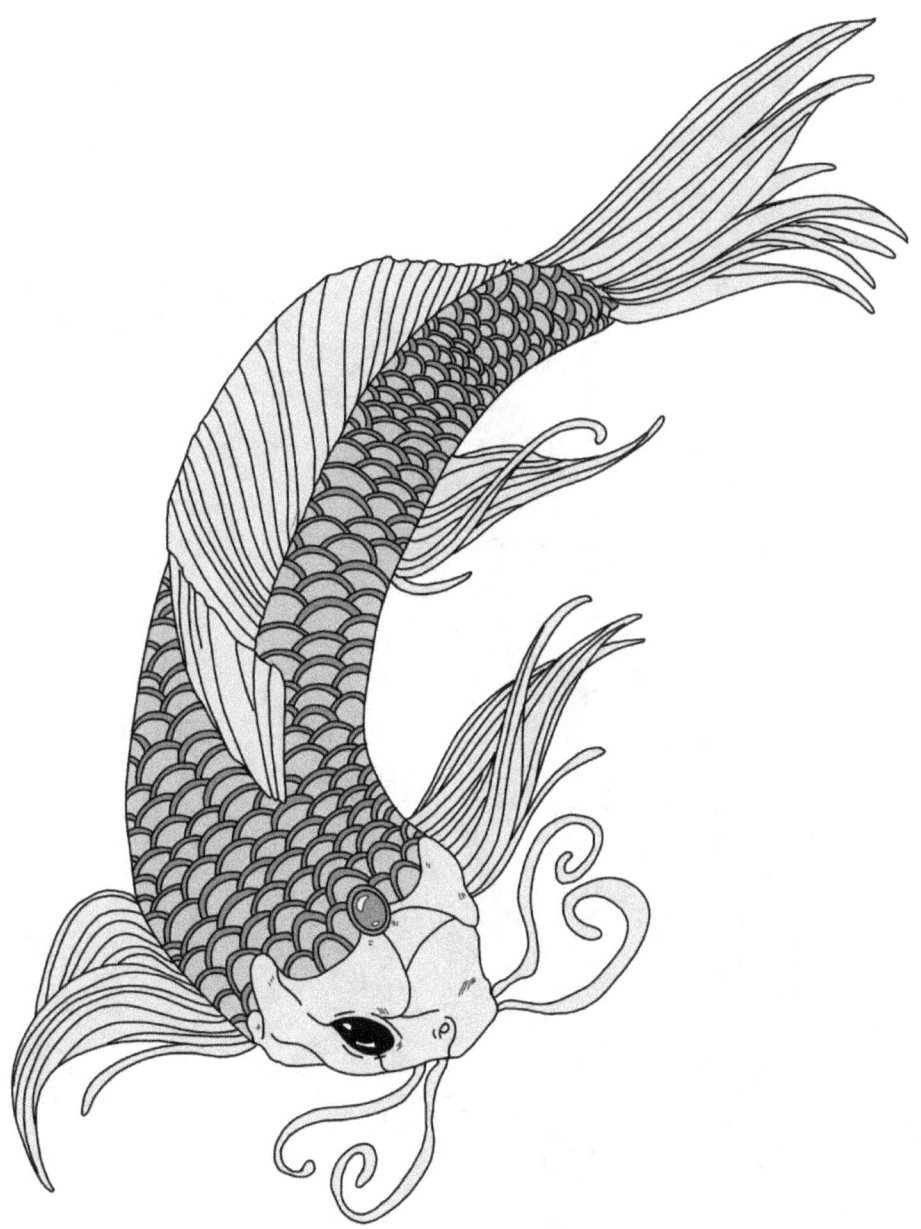

Our Koi is completely green, with a light purple for the jewel

on the head.

The fins and the head are a lighter green than the body is.

The extra lines inside the scales is are a darker green

Step 16.

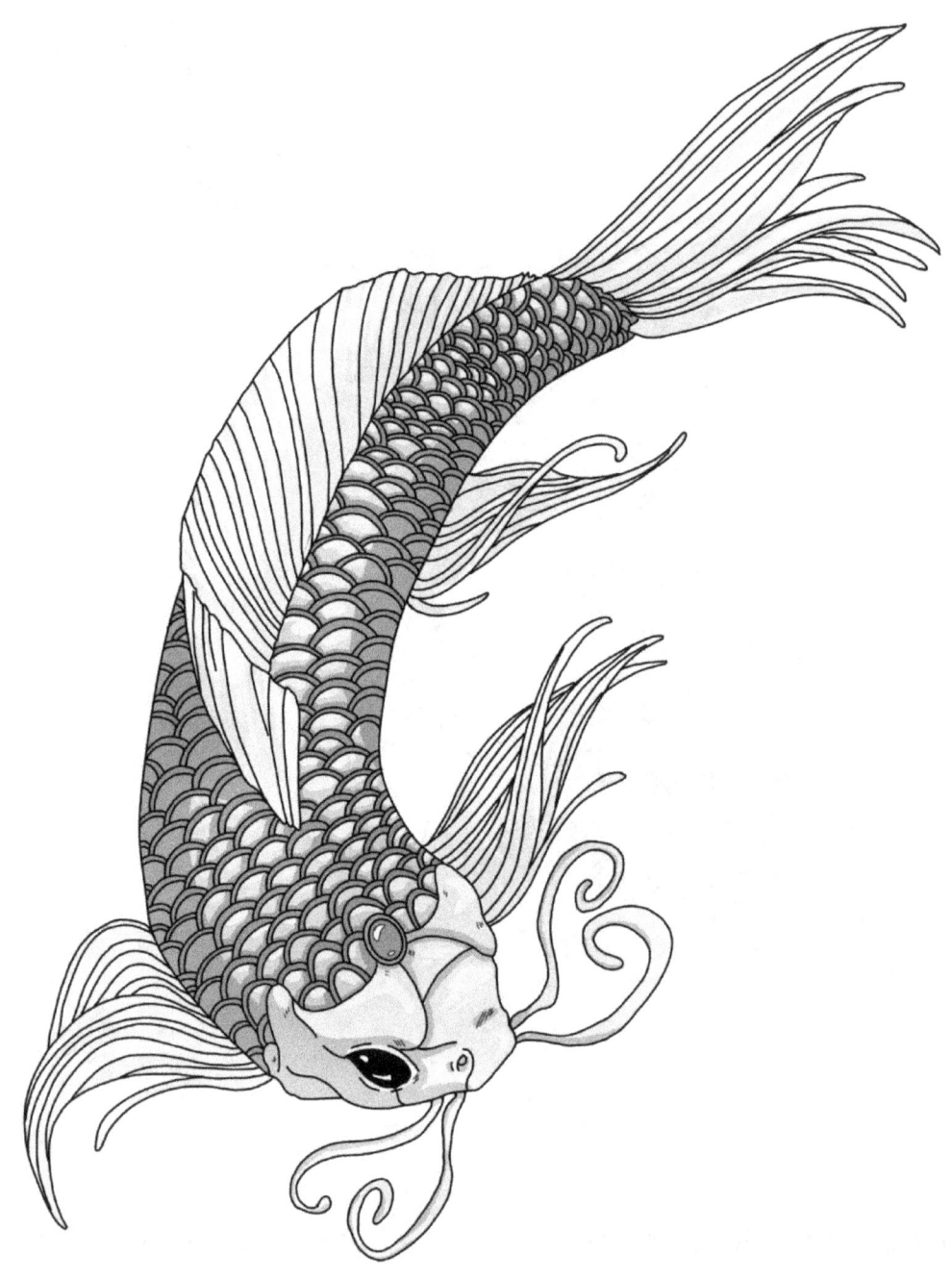

Add shadow and highlights to give our koi volume.

Step 17.

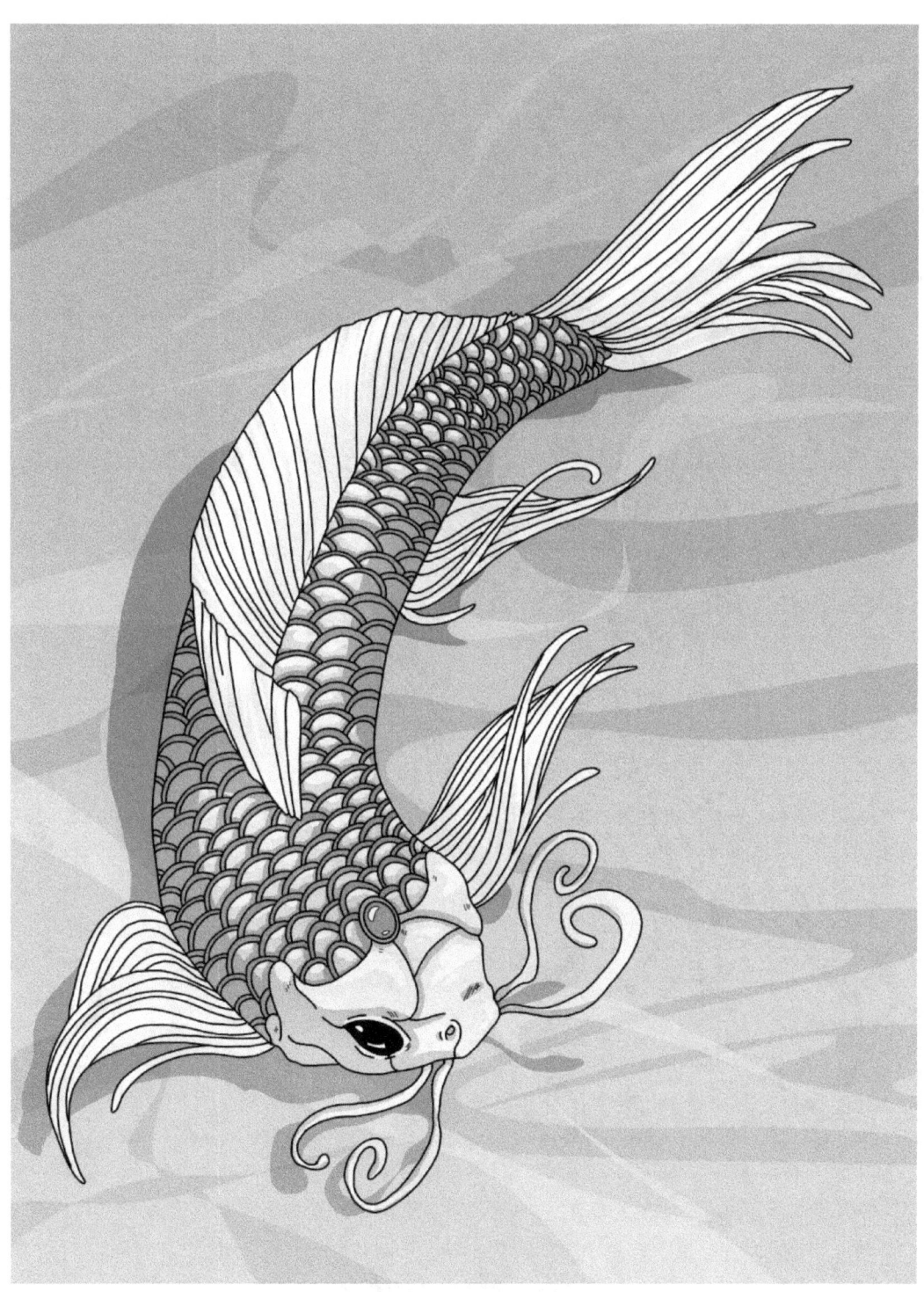

Colored version.

Step 18.

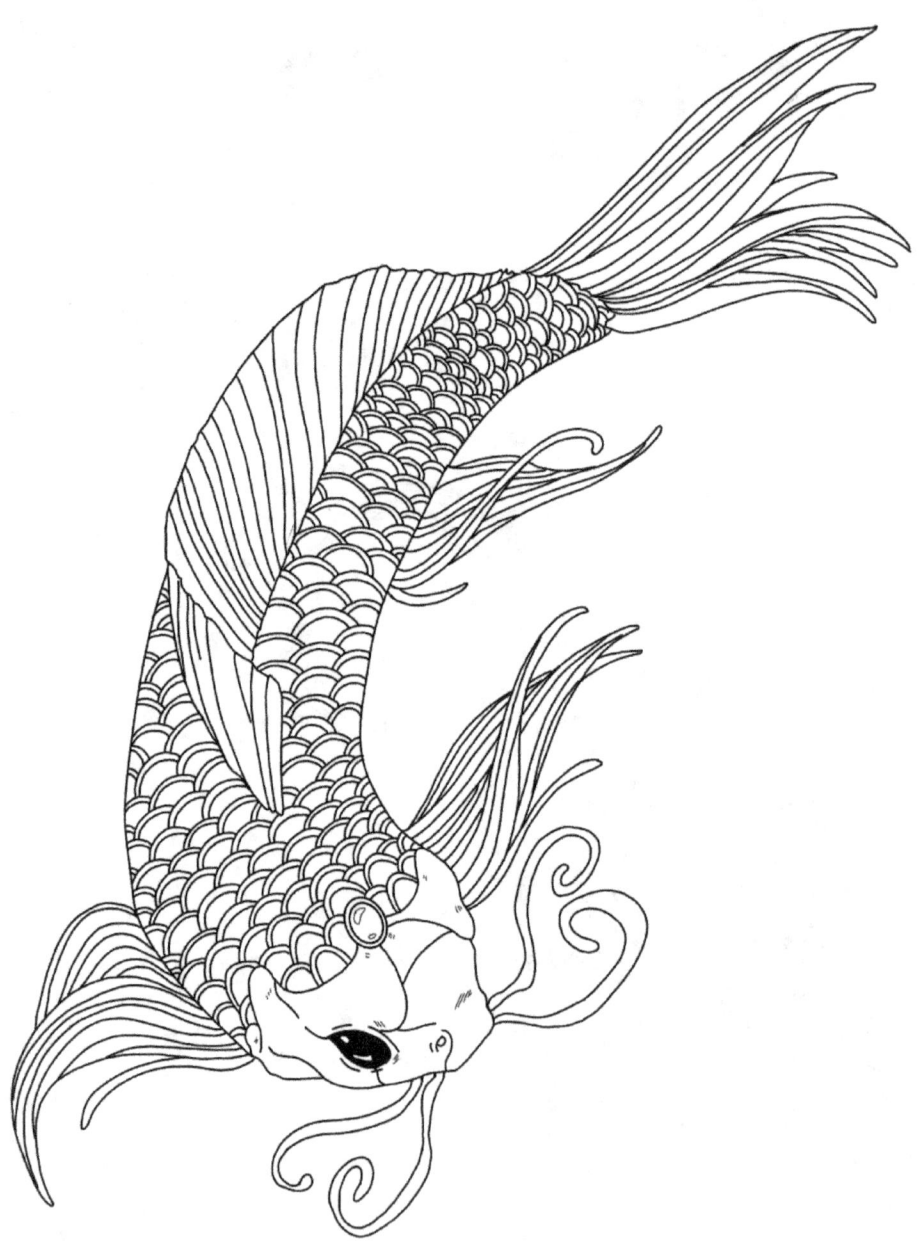

Line art version.

About the Author

Andy Hopper is an American illustrator born in sunny California just a hair's breadth from the beautiful Sierra foothills. After studying Design and Media at UCLA, Andy decided to try his hand at teaching his own unique style of art to novice artists just starting out with their craft.

He has won numerous art awards and has several publications in print and e-book to his credit. His e-books teach the beginner artist how to draw using simple techniques suitable for all ages. While Andy prefers using chalk, pencil and pastels for his own artwork, but has been known to dabble in the world of watercolour from time to time and teach this skill to his students.

Andy Hopper lives just outside of Los Angeles in Santa Monica, California with his wife of 15 years and their three children. His art studio is a welcome respite to the area and he has been known to start impromptu outdoor art sessions with the people in his neighborhood for no charge.